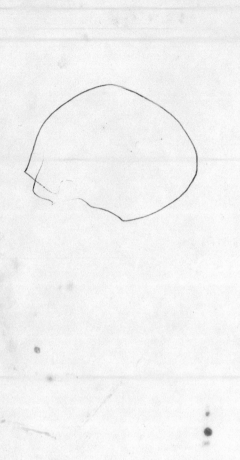

Compton's Precyclopedia

Based on The Young Children's Encyclopedia, published by
Encyclopaedia Britannica, Inc.

This is the letter **E**

"E" comes after "D" and before "F."

A small "e" looks different from a capital "E." eE

You can make a capital "E" by using a long straw and three ice-cream sticks.

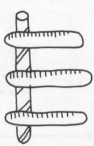

Here are some "e" things to do.

Eat a chocolate sundae.

Empty your pockets.

Enclose a letter in an envelope.

Enter a dark forest.

Escape from the forest.

Entertain your parents.

Now take an "e" walk. See how many things you can find inside and outside your house that have names beginning with "e."

Edith was excited about everything her eyes saw. So she exchanged

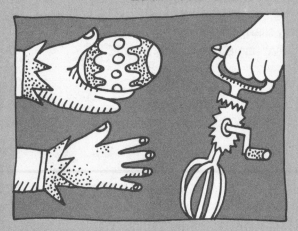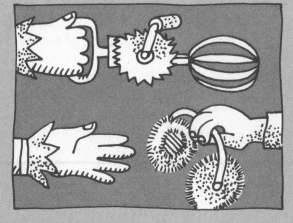

the Easter egg for an eggbeater...   *the eggbeater for earmuffs...*

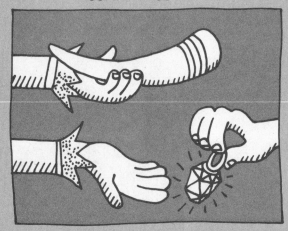

and the elephant tusk for an emerald...

which should have made her as wealthy as an empress.

an empty envelope for an eraser...

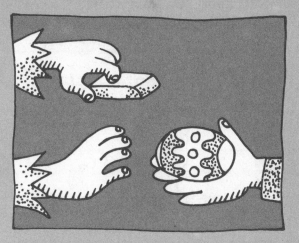

the eraser for an Easter egg...

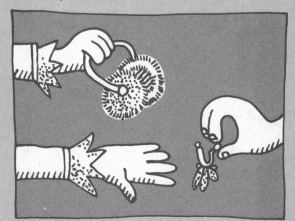

the earmuffs for an earring...

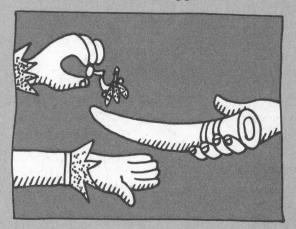

the earring for an elephant tusk...

But, of course, you know how Edith exaggerates!

Eight swift eagles fly in the skies,
Cut through the air with piercing cries,
Poke through the clouds, swoop to the ground,
Soar back up where they can't be found.

Eight proud eagles, flying high —
Can *you* find them in the sky?

The picture-words in this poem all rhyme with "free." Can you say the words?

Up in the meadow where the birds fly free,

I climbed up in a big green [tree]

I climbed to see what I could see

And felt a tickle on my [knee]

I looked to see what it could be.

It was a furry, buzzing [bee]

I climbed back down-ran from the [tree]

And hoped the [bee] would not sting me.

I think I'll climb another [tree]

And not that bee's . . . don't you agree?

Emily and the elephants

Early one evening an evil elf watched a train of circus cages going by. When the train stopped at a red light, the elf opened some of the cage doors. Eleven elephants escaped.

The eleven elephants went into the East Electric Company building. One climbed onto the escalator. Two others got stuck in the elevators. The doors started to close but the elephants' ears got caught.

Eight elephants stopped in the lobby and started to eat everything. One elephant brushed against a blackboard. He wiped everything off as if he were a big eraser. The elf enjoyed this.

Everyone ran from the elephants except Emily. She hooked her elbow through one elephant's trunk and led it to the door. Then she easily led each elephant outside one by one. She didn't even get excited when she told the elf, "Everyone has had enough of you and your elephants. We're eager for you to leave. "Exit!"

Can you find all the "e" words in this story? Can you find 11 elephants in the picture?

There are 5 things in this picture that are out of place. All of them begin with the letter "e." Can you find the 5 things?

The secret of the golden egg

The names of all the things in the pictures below start with "E." Can you name them?

If there was anything on 🌍 Earth that Ethel 🦅 Eagle wanted, it was to lay a golden 🥚 egg. One dark night as she was exploring the forest for food, she saw Edward 🧝 Elf. "Oh, Edward, you're just the 🧝 elf I want to see!" cried Ethel. "What's the problem, Ethel?" asked Edward. "I'm eager to lay a golden ☀️ egg," sighed Ethel, "but I don't know how." "No problem," said Edward and disappeared in a flash of ⚡ electricity. One evening Ethel was sitting in her nest when BANG! an enormous golden ☀️ egg suddenly appeared. "Edward 🧝 Elf has done it again," screeched Ethel. "But this can't be an eagle ☀️ egg," she thought. "It's too big. I'll just look up ○ 'Egg' in my *Compton's* 📖 *Encyclopedia* and see what kind of egg this could be." Ethel looked and looked. But she couldn't find an ☀️ egg as big as hers. And so Ethel sat on her golden  egg and waited. After several days she heard a

crack. And then another crack, much louder. And finally a noise

so loud it sounded like an earthquake. What do you think

popped out? A golden eagle? A golden eel?

A golden elf? WRONG! It was a beautiful golden baby

elephant with large soft eyes and big flapping

ears. And because Ethel Eagle was its mother,

the elephant learned how to fly. Now, have you ever

seen an elephant like that?

All about 5

Here are 5 drums.
Count them.

Here are 5 cars.
Count them.

Here are 5 cows.
Count them.

Is this a group of 5?
How many more of these
would you need to make 5?

Is this a group of 5?

Is this a group of 5?
How many more of these
would you need to make 5?

Draw 5 flowers, 5 dogs, 5 trees.

Can you find 5 of the same thing in this picture?

Do you remember?

How many fish are here?

How many fish are here?

How many fish are here?

How many fish are here?

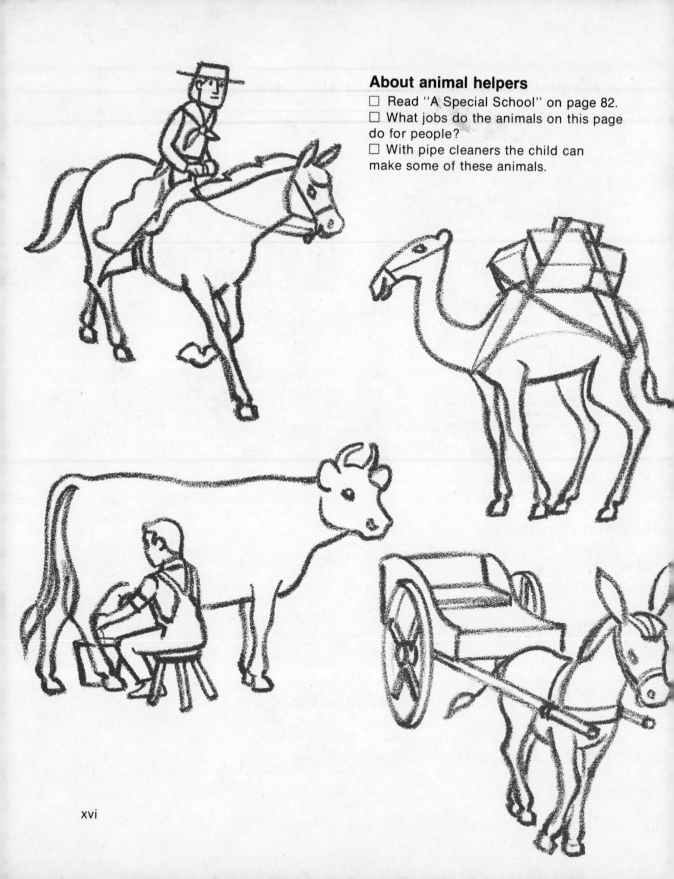

About animal helpers

☐ Read "A Special School" on page 82.
☐ What jobs do the animals on this page do for people?
☐ With pipe cleaners the child can make some of these animals.

xvii

About pretending

☐ Read "A Room Full of Yesterdays" on page 140.

☐ A group game. Fill a box with old hats, jewelry, dresses, coats, shoes, ties, and other clothing. Blindfold the children. Have each one pick out (in 30 seconds) five things to wear. Divide the group into two teams. Wearing the clothes they picked, each team must put on a play for the rest of the group.

About natural resources

☐ Read "The Boy Who Lives in a Snowhouse" on page 106.

Eskimos use the things around them for clothing, food, and shelter.

☐ Ask the child to imagine what it would be like if his family had to live in a forest using just the natural resources they could find.

☐ Have the child draw pictures showing:
The shelter they might build.
The clothes they might wear.
The food they might find and how they would cook it.

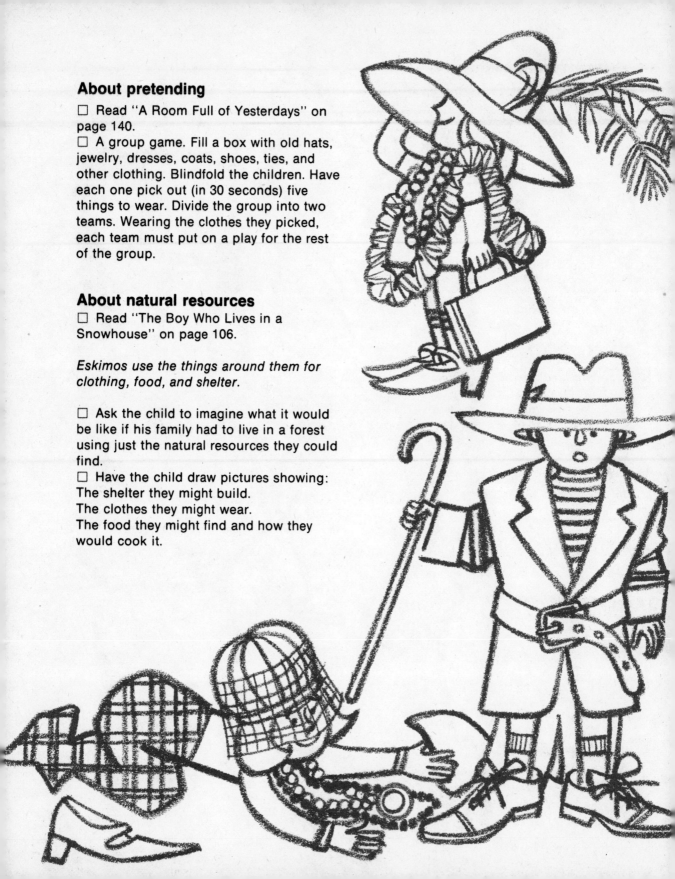

About exploring in the city

☐ Read "Do You Want to Be an Explorer?" on page 118.

☐ An exploring game. Here is a list of things for the child and his friends to hunt for in the park. Set a time limit. The one who finds the most is the winner.
A twig
A bird feather
A dandelion
A pinecone

☐ An exploring game in the yard. How many different kinds of insects, flowers, birds, trees, and other plants can the child see? Set a time limit.

More about exploring

☐ Before reading "Exploring with Animals" on page 124, ask the child if he can name the animals in the pictures.

☐ What kinds of transportation do people in this country use for exploring? (Walking; bicycling; riding in cars, boats, buses, subways, trains, airplanes)

☐ Talk with the child about the things we need as a result of so many different kinds of transportation. Why do we have so many sidewalks? Streets? Tunnels? Highways? Waterways? If we used only animals for exploring, would we need these things?

xix

About the Earth

☐ Read "Inside the Earth" on page 16.
☐ Questions about the Earth:*
How big is the Earth?
How much does the Earth weigh?

*For answers, see *Compton's Encyclopedia* article "Earth."

More about the Earth

☐ Read "Where on Earth?" on page 20.
☐ Look at the picture on page 22. Ask the child to point out the two coldest places on Earth and the hottest place on Earth. Can he name the animals that live near the North and South Poles? The animals that live near the Equator? The animals that live where it is warm part of the time and cold part of the time? What animals live near where the child lives?
☐ A riddle:
There was a house with four windows, one on each side. Each window faced south. One day a bear walked past. What kind of bear was it?
Answer:
A polar bear. (The house was at the North Pole, where the only direction is south.)

About buildings

☐ Read "Where Am I?" on page 64.
☐ Take a "building walk." Talk about the purposes of different buildings the child sees. (Apartment building, for homes; office building, for business; theater; church; a filtration plant, for cleaning water; museum; school)

About electricity

☐ Read "Electricity, Please" on page 72.
☐ Have the child look around his house and point out the things that would not work without electricity. Then ask the child to point out things outside the house that would not work without electricity.

For experiments showing how electricity works, see *Compton's Encyclopedia* article on "Electricity."

About responsibilities

☐ Read "How to Pick a Leader" on page 68.
☐ Talk about the responsibilities of the people who live in the child's house. What are his mother's responsibilities? His father's? His sisters' and brothers'? Ask the child what would happen if everyone in his house stopped doing the jobs they were supposed to do. (How would the house or apartment look? Who would buy and cook the food? Who would fix things when they break?)
☐ Talk about people who have responsibilities outside the house. (Who is responsible for making the town or city a safe place to live? Who is responsible for the roads? The mail? Schools?)

About people then and now

☐ Read "The Lost Necklace" on page 130.

People explore because they want to find answers to questions.

☐ Ask the child how he finds answers to questions. (Asks an adult, looks in a book, watches television, goes to the library, goes to school)

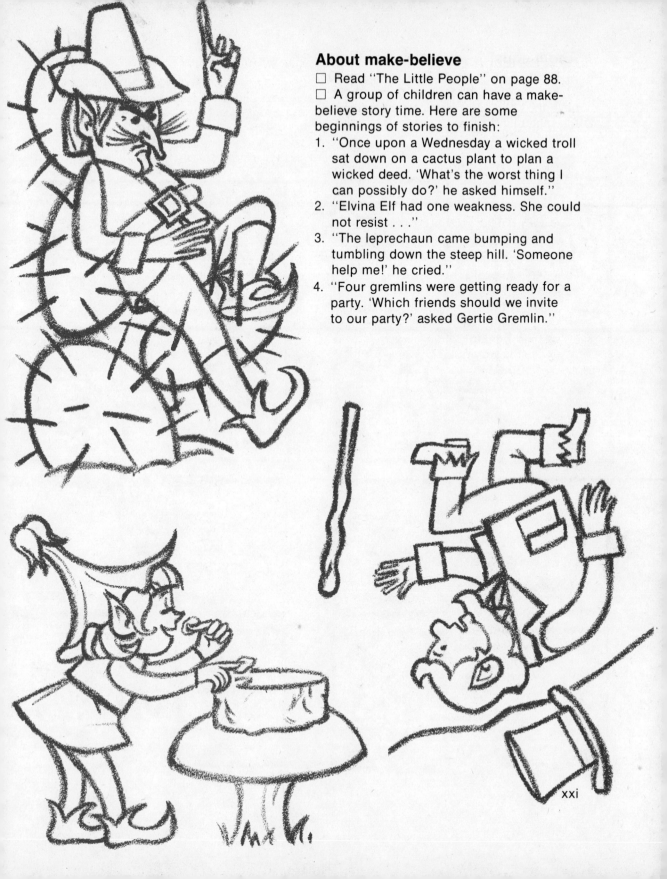

About make-believe

☐ Read ''The Little People'' on page 88.

☐ A group of children can have a make-believe story time. Here are some beginnings of stories to finish:

1. ''Once upon a Wednesday a wicked troll sat down on a cactus plant to plan a wicked deed. 'What's the worst thing I can possibly do?' he asked himself.''

2. ''Elvina Elf had one weakness. She could not resist . . .''

3. ''The leprechaun came bumping and tumbling down the steep hill. 'Someone help me!' he cried.''

4. ''Four gremlins were getting ready for a party. 'Which friends should we invite to our party?' asked Gertie Gremlin.''

xxi

About equal
☐ Read "Few Against Many" on page 102.
☐ Following the directions in the article, have the child select the correct picture for each blank square.

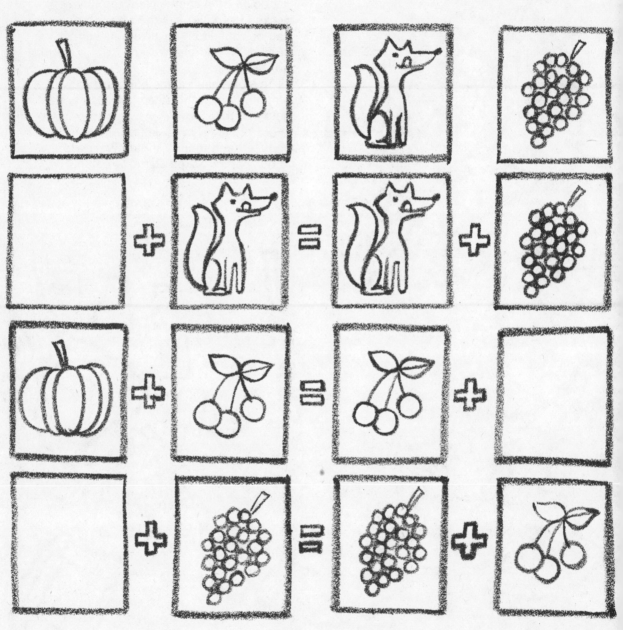

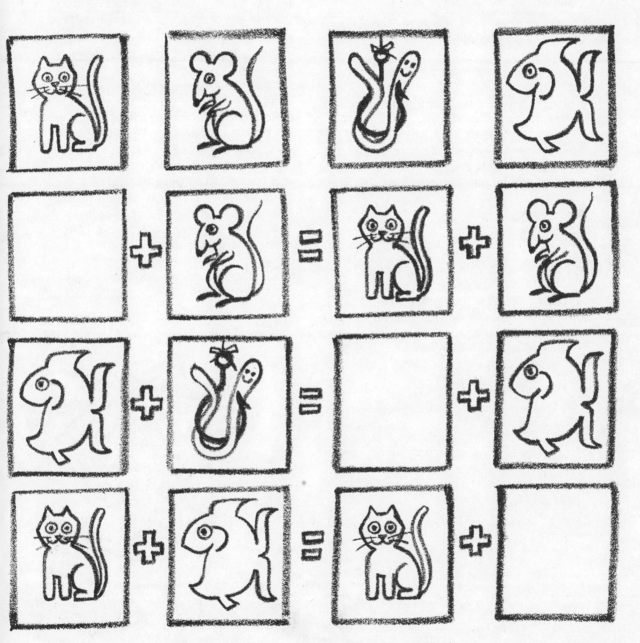

About sounds

☐ A riddle:
It can bounce, but it's not a ball.
It makes waves, but it's not water.
It can "see," but it has no eyes.
What is it?

For the answer, read "Sounds That See in the Dark" on page 34.

☐ Here are simple ways for the child to "feel" sound:
1. Touch a loudspeaker with fingertips and feel the sound vibrations.
2. Touch a piano or other stringed instrument when it is being played.
3. Sing a low note and feel the sound vibrations by putting fingers on throat.

About eggs

☐ Read "What's Inside?" on page 44.

Eggs come in many shapes and sizes.

☐ What eggs look like milk bottles?*
What eggs look like flower buds on the tips of stems?
What eggs look like bunches of grapes?
What egg is about 6 inches long and weighs almost 3 pounds?

*For answers, see *Compton's Encyclopedia* article "Egg."

About making an Easter-egg doll

☐ This project is for the older child. To make an Easter-egg doll he will need:

Uncooked egg	Paper
Straight pin	Glue
Crayons	Yarn
Scrap of felt cloth	Scissors

1. Carefully poke a hole at each end of egg with straight pin. (Make hole bigger at larger end of egg.)
2. Blow through small hole to get white and yolk out of egg.
3. Use crayons to make face at narrow end of egg. (Don't press too hard or eggshell will break.)
4. To make a skirt, cut felt to fit around egg. Glue felt to back of egg.
5. Cut pieces of yarn and glue on for hair.
6. Cut out paper strip. Fit strip around bottom of egg to make a stand. Glue ends of strip together.

The child can make several Easter-egg dolls and decorate them with different colors and costumes.

VOLUME **5**

Table of Contents   Volume 5

EAGLES Riders of the Wind, *pages 6-7*
Giant-sized birds that make soft noises and build nests big enough to hold people.

EARTH When the Earth Was New, *pages 8-9*

When People Thought the World Was Flat, *pages 10-15*
A make-believe king tries to sail off the edge of the world!

Inside the Earth, *pages 16-19*
Did you know that the inside of the earth is so hot that heavy tools may melt when they are used for digging deep into the ground?

Where on Earth?, *pages 20-25*

EARTHWORMS The Worm That Works like a Farmer, *pages 26-31*

EASTER ISLAND Where Am I?, *pages 32-33*
Giant statues stare at you from out of the ground. You are visiting a mysterious island in the Pacific Ocean.

ECHOES Sounds That See in the Dark, *pages 34-39*
How do echoes sometimes help people and animals see? Learn how ship captains— and even bats—use echoes.

ECLIPSES The Sky's Greatest Show, *pages 40-43*
It gets as dark as night in the middle of the day . . . animals are fooled and go to sleep . . . birds stop singing . . . what has caused these strange things to happen?

EGGS What's Inside?, *pages 44-49*
Many kinds of animals are hatched from eggs—how many can you name?

More About Eggs, *pages 50-51*

EGYPT Ancient Egypt, *pages 52-55*
Vast deserts . . . giant pyramids . . .
hundreds of treasures . . . the kingdom
of ancient Egypt.

Black Pharaohs of Ancient Egypt,
pages 56-59

Down the River to Cairo, *pages 60-63*
An adventure on the longest river in the
world!

EIFFEL TOWER Where Am I?, *pages 64-65*

EINSTEIN, ALBERT The Man Who Had the Answers,
pages 66-67
A famous scientist answers questions about
space and the stars and the whole universe
. . . questions that no one could answer before.

ELECTIONS How to Pick a Leader, *pages 68-71*

ELECTRICITY Electricity, Please, *pages 72-77*
What is electricity? Where does it come from?

A Shocking Fish, *pages 78-79*
This fish has so much electricity in it that it
has the power to knock down a horse!

More About Electricity, *pages 80-81*

ELEPHANTS A Special School, *pages 82-87*
Did you know that some elephants are
trained in special one-room schoolhouses?
They learn how to drag logs and pull up
trees—and as a reward they are given
bananas.

ELVES The Little People, *pages 88-93*

ENGLAND The Big Country on the Little Islands,
pages 94-99
Piccadilly Circus . . . kings and queens . . .
Robin Hood . . . a journey through England,
Scotland, Ireland, and Wales.

More About England, *pages 100-101*

EQUAL Few Against Many, *pages 102-103*
A first adventure with mathematics.

ERICSSON, LEIF Captain of the Dragon Ship, *pages 104-105*

ESKIMOS The Boy Who Lives in a Snowhouse,
pages 106-111
*Life in an igloo in a very cold part of the
world where polar bears and walruses live.*

ETHIOPIA Where Am I?, *pages 112-113*

EVEREST, MOUNT The Highest Climb, *pages 114-115*
*Brave men conquer the highest mountain in
the world . . . fighting snow and icy cliffs,
they climb until they're above the clouds.*

EVERGLADES Where Am I?, *pages 116-117*

EXPLORING Do You Want to Be an Explorer?,
pages 118-123
*Magellan is first to sail around the world . . .
Cortés explores Mexico . . . Peary reaches
the North Pole!*

Exploring with Animals, *pages 124-129*

The Lost Necklace, *pages 130-135*
A mystery about people of long ago.

Lenny, the Spelunker, *pages 136-139*
How would you like to explore a cave?

A Room Full of Yesterdays, *pages 140-143*

EYES AND EARS How Peter Found the Circus, *pages 144-147*

Eyes That Hear, Speech That's Seen,
pages 148-151
*Do you know that you would still be able to
understand other people if you were deaf?
You would have your own special language!*

Books to Touch and Books That Talk,
pages 152-155

Gail's Best Friend, *pages 156-159*

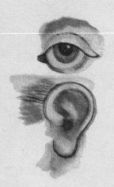

Here are more words beginning with "E" ... *and* ... **Here is where you may read about them**

Earthquake....................**Aquanauts**, *Book 1, page 114*

Earth, *Book 5, page 16*

Mountains, *Book 10, page 118*

Edison, Thomas................**Light**, *Book 9, page 86*

Eel..............................**Electricity**, *Book 5, page 78*

Elizabeth, Queen...............**London**, *Book 9, page 152*

Emperor.......................**Napoleon Bonaparte**, *Book 11, page 14*

Peter the Great, *Book 12, page 72*

Empress.......................**Peking**, *Book 12, page 42*

Engine.........................**Railroads**, *Book 13, page 34*

Equator........................**Earth**, *Book 5, page 20*

Explosives.....................**Dynamite**, *Book 4, pages 154 to 159*

Riders of the Wind

If this eagle spread its wings in your room, it would take up as much space as your bed. Yet this heavy bird flies easily, sometimes using air currents to ride the wind.

Eagles build huge nests of sticks (big enough to hold people!) on rocky cliffs and use the same nest year after year.

When there are eggs to hatch, both the mother and father eagles take turns sitting on them. And both parents care for the little eagles afterward, bringing them mice, fish, rabbits, ducks, snakes, or squirrels to eat. But eagles don't always catch their own food. Sometimes they steal it from another bird by chasing it high in the sky until the tired bird drops the food it is carrying in its beak.

You would expect such a big bird to make a big sound. But the eagle's sound is a kind of squealing, not nearly so loud and fierce as you'd expect.

If an eagle has to protect itself, it uses its hooked beak and strong claws. Its claws can go through the toughest skin.

This bird has very good eyesight, too. Even when it is so high in the air that it can hardly be seen, the eagle can see small things on the ground.

Eagles do not all look alike. A golden eagle wears a cap of gold feathers. A bald eagle is not really bald. It looks that way because its head feathers are white. Some eagles have "boots" of feathers all the way down to their claws. Others have just plain naked legs.

Pictures of eagles appear on coins and seals. But real eagles are getting scarce, and now there are laws to save the ones that are left.

If you like learning about Birds,
read about them in Volume 2.

When the Earth Was New

People have always wondered how the Earth was made. We still don't know how for sure. Maybe our Earth was once part of the sun. Maybe it broke away to become our Earth.

One thing that we do know is that a long time ago the Earth was hot, inside and out. There was nothing living on the Earth then. It was too hot. The Earth was just a boiling ball of soft stuff.

The Earth flamed and boiled for a very long time. Then . . . slowly . . . slowly . . . it began to cool. It took a long time before it was cool enough for oceans to form and life to start. But once life did start, it filled the oceans and covered the land.

Millions of years later, there came an animal who could think. An animal who could think and find out what the Earth was like before there was any life on it—maybe even what things were like before there *was* any Earth!

We call this animal *man*.

If you're interested in learning about the Earth,
look under Land and Water *in Volume 9*
and Ocean *in Volume 11.*

9

When People Thought the World Was Flat

There was a time when people thought the world was flat. They felt certain that ships sailing too far would fall off the edge. They laughed at men who said the world was round, even when the men told them why they thought so.

But today almost everyone knows that the world is round.

This is a poem about a make-believe king who thought the world was flat and tried to sail off the edge.

The Ship That Tried to Sail Off the Earth

"I quit!" said the king. "There's nothing to do;
    Everything's old, and nothing is new.
I've seen all the players; I know all of their names;
    I'm tired of hunting and fighting and games.
I'm going to live in a cave on the slope,
    Unless you've a better idea—I hope."

"That's silly," the quick-thinking jester replied.
    "To hide in a cave is not dignified.
A person who finds himself royal at birth
    Should do something grand, like sail off the Earth."
The king asked his wise men what they thought of that.
    "You could," they replied, "for the world is quite flat."

"My lords," said the king, "this is fine sailing weather.
    We'll sail to the edge, and we'll go off together."
He asked who was coming . . . the answers were slow.
    It seemed that not many were anxious to go.
So he ordered the peasants to join him at sea,
    And a band of musicians—as scared as could be.

11

The music was sad, and the peasants were white;
    As they waved a good-bye, the ship sailed out of sight.
"Head straight for the edge!" said the king to the crew,
    Who started to cry—and the peasants did, too.
And then the musicians all started to bawl
    While playing sad songs and expecting to fall.

But after a day they got tired of crying,
    And after a week they were not even sighing.
Then just when they weren't quite so sad anymore,
    They ran out of food; so they pulled into shore.
"We can't stay too long!" said the king, with a glare.
    But the end of the week found them still anchored there.

The people were friendly; their music was gay.
    They sang and they danced in a strange bouncy way.
Their food was delicious; their clothes made with string.
    They taught all their games to the visiting king.
But then he grew restless and boarded the ship
    With all of his men for the rest of the trip.

"When I make my mind up," the king told his crew,
    "My mind is made up! So there's nothing to do
But sail to the edge!" he cried. "And be quick!"
    The crew members sniffled; the peasants felt sick.
The frightened musicians could not keep the tune.
    They all had a feeling the end would be soon.

But the sunshine grew warm, and the breezes blew sweet,
    And they sailed till they ran out of something to eat.
Then they stopped to get food, and they all stayed on shore
    Till the king gave the word; then they'd sail off once more.
And each of the countries was different and fun,
    And they visited many before they were done.

12

Then one starry evening right after they dined,
    The king told his men, "I am quite sad, I find.
Though this trip seems to grow more exciting each day,
    And I wish we could go on forever this way,
I've got a strange feeling the edge is quite near.
    Drop anchor till morning," he said with a tear.

The sun in the morning showed land to one side
    And a big crowd of people! "We're home!" the king cried.
"It's the king!" said the lords. "But where have you been?
    Can you sail off the Earth and get back on again?"
"Not at all," said the king. "We went sailing and found
    That the Earth has no edge, for we sailed clear around.

"And though from the start we expected to fall,
    We learned from our trip that the world is a ball!"
The people all cheered, but the wise men would not.
    They said, "The world's flat, as we always have taught!"
But the wonderful tales from the men on the ship
    Convinced all the others they'd made such a trip.

Inside the Earth

What is the boy in this picture sitting on?

He's sitting on a *chair*. But that's not all he's sitting on. Under the chair is a *rug*. Under the rug is a *floor*. Under the floor is a *cellar*. Under the cellar is the *ground*.

But that's not all!

Under the ground that is under the cellar that is under the floor that is under the rug that is under the chair that is under the boy is the rest of the Earth.

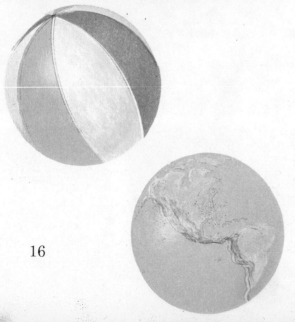

We know what the outside of the Earth looks like. From far out in space it looks something like a ball. No one has ever had a chance to look very far *inside* the Earth. But we think we know some of the things we would find if we could.

16

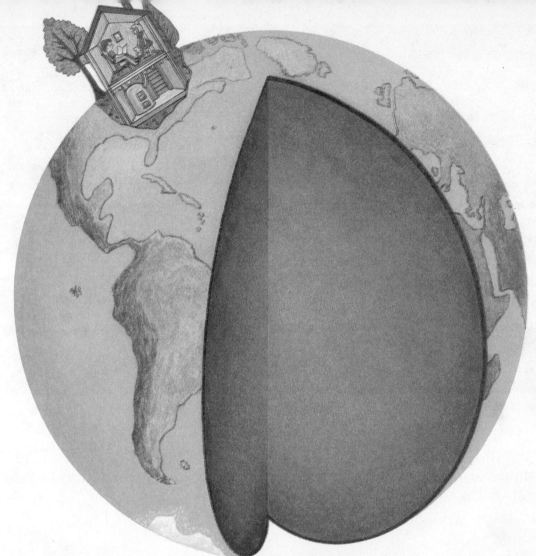

If the inside of the Earth really is the way these scientists think it is—and if it could be sliced like a melon or a peach—it would look like this.

Most scientists believe that the Earth is filled with layers of rock, one on top of another. In the center, or middle, there is probably a ball—or *core*—of metal that is mostly iron.

The deepest hole we have been able to dig into our very solid Earth is more than four miles deep.

A hole that would show us for sure what's in the very middle of the Earth would have to be about 4,000 miles deep.

Our four-mile-deep holes have proved *something*. They have proved that the deeper we dig or drill a hole, *the hotter it gets*. The temperature at the bottom of a four-mile hole is hot enough to boil water. Deeper down, the Earth is still hotter. It is so hot that if we went far enough, the tools that were doing the digging would melt!

Because the inside of the Earth is so hot, we'll probably never learn about it by drilling holes. Fortunately, there are other ways to learn.

A *volcano* looks like a mountain stuffed with exploding fireworks. It shoots out fire and smoke and rocks. Some of the rocks inside the volcano are so hot that they melt. This melted rock, or *lava*, runs out like thick chocolate and spreads all around. After the lava has cooled, scientists can learn a lot about what's inside the Earth by looking carefully at the melted rock that poured out of the volcano.

There is still another way to learn about what's inside the Earth.

18

Sometimes a big layer of rock that is deep, deep down slips and rubs against another layer of rock. This causes a shaking and rumbling called an *earthquake.*

Scientists learn something about what's inside the Earth by using special earthquake instruments.

What's inside the Earth is a riddle. Nature gives us some hints when volcanoes shoot out melted rock and when there are earthquakes. It lets us know that in some places there is solid rock, and in other places hot melted rock, and in still other places hot melted iron. But we still need to know a lot more than we do. When you grow up, you might be the one who will tell us exactly what is under the ground that is under the cellar that is under the floor that is under the rug that is under the chair where the boy is sitting!

Want to know more?
Read Fossils *in Volume 6 and* Volcanoes *in Volume 16.*

Where on Earth?

Why can't you climb the North Pole?

Because there isn't any pole there for you to climb.

The North Pole and the South Pole are the names of two places on Earth.

If you look at a globe, you can see that they are as far apart as they can get and still be on the same globe.

If you don't like to go to bed at night, you'd like to be at the North Pole or the South Pole. Daylight at either pole lasts *six months*—and that's *half* of a *whole year!*

There's just one problem. The night lasts for six months, too. When either pole is having daylight, the other is in darkness. So if you could start from one of the poles just before it got dark and fly quickly enough to the other pole, you could always be in daylight!

Children who live in lands where the daylight lasts for several months have to sleep while the sun is shining. No one could stay awake until it got dark.

20

People don't live at either of the poles. It's much too cold. If you *had* to live at one of them, it would be hard to decide which one to pick.

The South Pole is the coldest place on Earth and is very windy. All of the land there is covered with very deep snow and ice.

But that might be better than living at the North Pole, because the North Pole is in the middle of the frozen Arctic Ocean!

Eskimos and many kinds of animals—reindeer, polar bears, wolves, and white rabbits, to name just a few—live on the land around the Arctic Ocean. In the waters around the North Pole are seals, sharks, walruses, and whales.

Probably the best-known animal at the South Pole is the funny-looking bird that some people think looks like a restaurant waiter —the penguin.

If you left the land around the North Pole to go to the South Pole, it would get warmer as you went . . . until you got about halfway there. Then it would start getting cooler again until you reached the very cold South Pole.

When you were halfway between the poles you would be at a place named the Equator. Just as there are no poles to let you know when you're at the poles, there is no line around the world to let you know you're at the Equator. No signs, no anything. It is just the place halfway between the two poles.

The land at the Equator is hot and wet. Sometimes it rains there for days and days. Tall trees with broad leaves that are always green grow so close together that it is hard to find a way between them. Coconuts grow there, as well as delicious fruits, such as bananas and mangoes. Plants grow on the trunks of trees, and vines hang from the branches.

Wild monkeys swing through the trees. Parrots, red and green and yellow, make more noise than ten children shouting. Striped tigers and spotted leopards and giant snakes live there, too.

Do you know someone who takes ballet lessons? Maybe you do. An easy way to picture how the poles and the Equator move as the Earth spins is to think of the Earth as a ballerina.

As she spins on one toe, the tip of her crown is the North Pole, the toe she spins on is the South Pole, and the edge of her whirling skirt is the Equator.

Of course, you'd have to pull the floor away from her because the Earth spins through space.

Most of the world's people live where it isn't too hot or too cold—somewhere between the poles and the Equator.

But because men have always wanted to know about the dangerous, hard-to-reach parts of the world, they kept on trying to reach the poles and explored the hot jungles of the Equator. Some explorers were killed by wild animals or jungle men. Some died of jungle fevers.

In the Arctic Ocean near the North Pole, a ship sometimes got caught in the ice. Sometimes the men ran out of food before summer weather melted the ice enough to let their ship get away.

Because early explorers were brave enough to start out for places they knew nothing about, we know a lot about the poles and the Equator. And when anyone asks, "Where on Earth can we find people?" we can answer, "You might find them anywhere."

The Worm That Works like a Farmer

Cynthia let go of Grandpa's hand long enough to cover her ears as the big bulldozer rumbled by. The ground shook a little as it passed.

Grandpa bent and picked up something from the ground.

Cynthia peeked into his big hand, and there was a sleek, fat earthworm. Cynthia watched it move back and forth.

"It's wiggling!" she cried, as Grandpa gently placed it on the ground.

"Back to work, little fellow," Grandpa said, playfully.

"Work?" asked Cynthia. "How do worms work?"

26

"When worms burrow through the earth, they help keep it loose and rich. Of course, the worms don't know it, but this rich, loose soil is useful for the farmer."

Just then Cynthia saw a hungry robin tugging fiercely at an earthworm.

"Look, Grandpa, the robin pulled so hard the worm broke! Will there be two worms for the robin now?"

"No," Grandpa said, "but the part that's left in the ground may grow a new part to make up for the part the robin ate."

"How does the worm hold on so tightly?" Cynthia asked.

"Let's go home and get my magnifying glass," answered Grandpa, "and I'll show you."

As they crossed the sidewalk, they saw a few more earthworms that had been turned up by the bulldozer. The worms seemed to be sunning themselves, but Grandpa explained that since earthworms can't see, they were having a hard time finding their *burrows*, or holes, in the ground.

"If they don't get into the cool earth pretty soon, they'll die," Grandpa said. "The sun is a great enemy of theirs. So is a heavy rain, which might flood their holes and drown them."

At home Cynthia ran into the house and got the large magnifying glass.

Grandpa turned a spadeful of dirt at the edge of the garden. It was full of earthworms. Cynthia looked at one through the magnifying glass.

"It looks big," she said. "What are those things sticking out all over its body?"

"Bristles," Grandpa said, "that are something like those on your hairbrush. When a robin finds a worm, the worm pushes the bristles into the dirt and holds tight. It takes a lot of pulling to get the worm out."

While Cynthia watched through the glass, Grandpa explained that earthworms also use the bristles to help them move from place to place.

"Next time you're at the beach," he said, "try wriggling along in the sand using your hands and feet. Then you'll have some idea about the way worms move. You'll use your hands and feet to push you along the way the worm uses its bristles."

29

When she thought of playing earthworm at the beach, Cynthia laughed. "But, Grandpa," she teased, "if I were an earthworm I'd still get hungry. How would I eat?"

"If you were an earthworm," Grandpa said, "you'd have a lip like a thick little shovel. You'd use this lip for digging through the ground. You'd really be eating your way through the earth. You'd eat earth to get the tiny bit of vegetable and animal matter that is in it.

"Look at the tiny hills all around us on the ground. Those are called *worm castings*. The worms have brought up soil they ate under the ground. After the soil has gone through the worm's body, the soil is richer and things grow better in it."

Grandpa smiled. "In a way worms are farmers themselves. They pull seeds underground that may grow into trees and bushes. Worms also pull dead leaves, small bones, sticks, and bits of grass down into their burrows. Slowly, these become part of the dirt and help make soil richer and better for growing things. The earthworm tunnels let air and water into the soil, and that helps things grow, too."

Cynthia took one last look at the little worm disappearing into the soft ground.

"Earthworms are so valuable to gardeners," Grandpa said, "that some people have earthworm farms. They grow earthworms and ship them all over the world to places where there aren't enough earthworms."

"Earthworms sound very busy," said Cynthia. "If I were an earthworm, I think I'd be tired."

Where Am I?

How would you like to visit an island far away in the ocean where great statues seem to stare at you wherever you look? Statues as high as tall trees!

Some of the statues are just enormous heads. Others show the upper bodies of people. They are made of stone, and no one knows for sure who made them. They are all stuck in the ground, almost as if they grew there. But they didn't—they were moved there.

The people who were living on this island when it was discovered more than 200 years ago made up stories about the giant statues—where they had come from and who had made them.

On the island are wooden tablets—wooden boards with writing on them. The writing is not like any we know—there are pictures of people, birds, fish, and plants, and some pictures that seem to be just designs. Who were the people who lived here long ago? Are these statues of important people? Most of the huge heads were made flat to hold heavy crowns. Are they statues of ancestors or of gods?

Stone-cutting tools have been found on the island. Cavemen used such tools, but cavemen didn't live in houses, and there are ancient houses on the island. Some of the houses are made of stones fitted together like a jigsaw puzzle. Nothing but the joints makes them stick together. There are stones so big and heavy that it must have taken many, many men to get them into place.

Someone, sometime, worked very hard to help make these statues and buildings. And you can see them today if you travel on a boat or airplane to Easter Island in the Pacific Ocean.

Look under Where Am I? *in Volume 16 and find Easter Island on the map.*

Sounds That See in the Dark

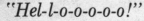

"Hel-l-o-o-o-o-o!"

The boy smiles. He hears the echo coming from the hills. Maybe it will talk to him.

"Echo, talk to me," the boy calls.

". . . to me," repeats the echo. *". . . to me . . . to me . . . to me."*

"Please, Echo, talk to me!" the boy tries again.

". . . to me." Again the echo repeats only his last words.

After a few more tries the boy shrugs and goes away.

Echoes simply repeat sounds. They can't say anything that we don't say. But let's pretend that echoes can talk back. Let's see what an echo might say if we asked it some questions.

"What are you, Echo?"

"I am the sound that you made. I am bouncing back to you from these hills."

"But, Echo, how can a sound bounce? A sound is not a ball."

"No, a sound is not a ball. A sound is a wave in the air. If you could see air the way you can see water, you'd see the waves that sounds make."

"And sound waves bounce?"

"Only if they hit something big and solid like the side of a hill or the walls of a cave or the walls of an empty house."

"What if nothing stops the sound waves?"

"They just go on getting smaller and smaller, or else the sound waves stop when they run into soft things like carpets and draperies or large pieces of furniture."

"My house has things like that. I guess that's why I never hear an echo in it. I'd like to take you home with me."

"I don't think you'd like an echo in your house. Echoes make lots of extra noise. We are not welcome in homes or offices or theaters. But there are some places where we are useful."

"Useful? You're the only echo that's useful. Real echoes don't answer questions. How can they be useful?"

"Real echoes can help people and animals 'see' in the dark."

"How can echoes help people and animals 'see'?"

Here is how echoes help bats "see." Even in pitch-black caves bats can fly where they want to go, never bumping into anything, and even catching tiny insects in the air. They can do this because, as they fly, bats keep making tiny, whistle-like sounds. These sounds bounce back to them from a cave wall or a flying insect, or almost anything else. The direction from which the echoes come and the time it takes the echoes to return tell the bats exactly where things are as they fly.

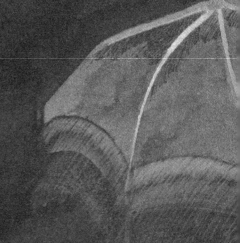

People can "see with sound," too.

Sometime you might go for a ride on a boat at a place where the fog is gray and thick. Let's say there are high rock cliffs near the place where the captain wants to land his boat.

The captain blows a horn and listens. He turns the boat a little one way or another and blows the horn again and listens. He keeps doing this until the boat floats safely in between the rock cliffs.

When he couldn't see with his eyes, how did the captain know where to make the boat go without hitting the rocks? Like the bats, he could tell by the echoes. By the way they sounded, and by how fast the echoes returned, he could tell how close he was to the cliffs.

Some echoes are so tiny and faint that we can't hear them with our ears. So men have invented a wonderful machine, an echo machine, that "hears" for them. With an echo machine, or *sonar*, we can find many things that are hidden under the water or under the land.

With *sonar* we can find icebergs in the darkness and fog. Icebergs are dangerous. Before echo machines were invented, many ships bumped into icebergs and were wrecked.

Now ships that sail through icy seas have an echo machine. It sends sound waves ahead into the water. If these sound waves bump into an iceberg, they bounce back as echoes. The sailors can't hear them, but by "reading the machine" the sailors on the ship can tell if icebergs are there, even when they can't see them.

Want to know more? Read about Bats *in Volume 2.*

The Sky's Greatest Show

Once upon a time—so the story goes—an explorer was captured by a tribe of natives in the jungle. The jungle people had no books or television or radio. They didn't even know that there was anything different in the world from the trees and the vines and the muddy rivers of their jungle. They were afraid of the explorer, and so they locked him up in a wooden cage.

"Let me out," the explorer said, "or I'll make the sun go away. Right here in the middle of the day I'll make something in the sky eat up your sun."

The jungle people didn't believe him. They laughed and poked sticks at him through the bars of the cage.

"All right," he said, "you'll see. My magic is strong. Now I'll make the sun go away in the middle of the day."

And the sun did go away! At least it seemed to. Something seemed to eat up the sun a little at a time until it was all gone, and the day was as dark as midnight.

The jungle people moaned and cried. They were very much afraid of this explorer whose magic was strong enough to take their sun away.

"Make the sun come back," they cried, "and we'll do anything you say. We'll set you free and give you food and great treasure."

"All right," the explorer said, "I'll make the sun come back."

And the sun did come back after a little while.

Do you know why it "went away" in the first place? And why it "came back"?

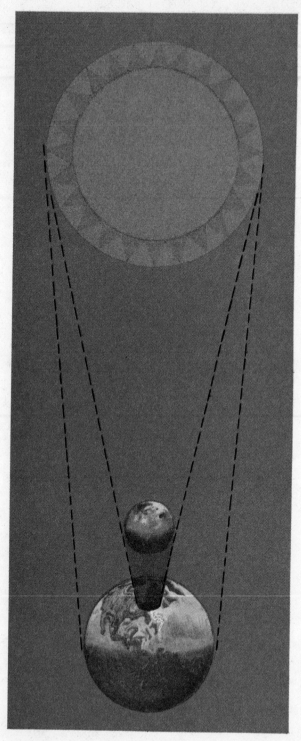

It really can turn as dark as night—right in the middle of the day. This happens when the sun is *eclipsed* by the moon. *Eclipse* means to hide something by coming in front of it.

You know that the moon goes around the Earth. And that the Earth and moon together go around the sun. Once in a while, as they all move, the moon gets between the sun and the Earth. That stops the sun's light from reaching part of the Earth. It gets dark in the daytime, and we say that there is an eclipse of the sun.

Scientists who study the sky can tell when these eclipses will happen. The explorer in our story knew there would be an eclipse. So he pretended to the jungle people that *he* made it happen.

When the moon comes between the sun and the Earth, the sun looks thinner and thinner until— almost as if somebody flicked off a light switch—the day becomes as dark as night. Even the animals are fooled. Birds stop singing, and hens go clucking to their roosts, thinking it is time to sleep.

Eclipses of the moon also happen but in a different way.

When the Earth gets in front of the sun, it throws a long black shadow over the moon. But some sunlight "leaks" through to the moon; so it never turns black, only a dull coppery color.

Eclipses of the sun or the moon don't happen often. The next time the sun is eclipsed where you live and it suddenly gets dark, don't be fooled and go to bed in the middle of the day like the chickens.

Even though the sun is darkened during an eclipse, never stare at it. There are still enough harmful rays to hurt your eyes.

Did you like this story?
Read about the Moon *in Volume 10*
and the Sun *in Volume 14.*

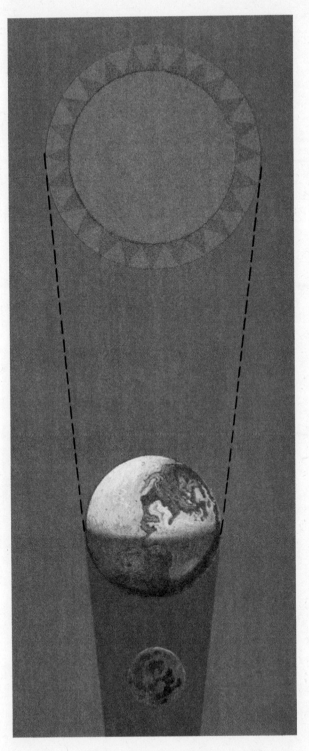

What's Inside?

When we think of eggs, we usually think of birds' eggs. But such animals as lizards and salamanders also come from eggs.

Or an egg may have a snake inside.

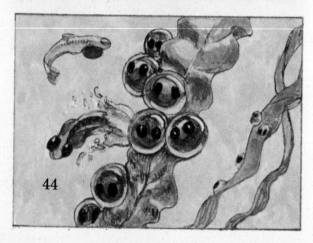

44

Many fish start out in eggs, too—in tiny eggs without hard shells.

Some eggs are so small that you wouldn't know they were there unless you had a magnifying glass.

This mother fish is a *perch*.

And on these strips of jelly—her underwater nest—are hundreds and hundreds of tiny eggs. A tiny piece of her nest could hold as many eggs as there are grains in a heaping tablespoonful of sugar.

Even baby dinosaurs poked
and pushed their way out of eggs.
These creatures lived millions of
years ago and were the largest
animals ever to walk on Earth—
yet some of them were born from
eggs not much larger than a
cucumber! Some of the eggs were
round like circles and were laid
in nests that were built in the
sand. The shells of the eggs felt
almost like leather.

Not very long ago, scientists
made a famous discovery of
dinosaur eggs in the Gobi Desert
in Mongolia in Asia. The eggs
they found had the bones of
unhatched dinosaurs inside.

It is believed that certain furry
animals may have eaten dinosaur
eggs millions of years ago and
that this is one reason there
aren't any dinosaurs anymore.

These aren't dinosaur eggs. They're robin eggs. The warm body of the mother robin covers each egg when she sits on the nest. If the eggs are not kept warm, the baby birds growing inside will die. So the mother bird sits and sits and sits.

One day she feels a bump. Then come stronger bumps . . . and still stronger *bumps* . . . until there's a BUMP that almost pushes the mother bird out of the nest. Now this is what she sees.

At first there's just a crack, going this way and that. Then the crack in the egg widens into a hole—not a smooth, round one but an every-which-way hole. A busy little beak, pecking and pushing, makes the hole grow and *grow* and GROW.

And then, at last, the baby bird is out of its shell.

48

Some eggs are as blue as the sky.

Others are as pink as a sunset.

Still others are speckled and freckled with color.

Some birds lay their eggs on the ground. Often these eggs match the colors of the ground so that other hungry animals won't find them.

When an animal comes out of its egg, it may be protected and fed by its parents for a while, but soon it will leave their protection. It, too, will become a parent and have eggs of its own to care for.

Did you like this story?
Look up Babies *in Volume 2.*

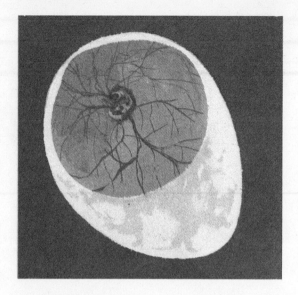
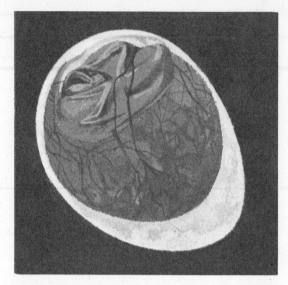

More About Eggs

When a baby chicken starts to grow inside an egg, it is nothing more than a tiny spot. Three weeks later, just before it breaks out of its shell, the chick fills the whole egg. You can see that it has done a lot of growing!

The chick floats in a bag of watery stuff, or *liquid*. The liquid keeps the chick from drying out and makes it easier for it to exercise its tiny muscles.

You might say that the chick has its lunch with it in a bag called the *yolk sac*. The yolk sac holds the yolk of the egg. The yolk is food that the chick uses while it is growing inside the eggshell. Another bag is like a small bathroom and catches the wastes from the growing chick.

There is a small air pocket at one end of the eggshell. A week before the chick is ready to crack its way out of the shell, it sticks its head under its wing and points its beak at the air pocket. Then, just two days before it is hatched, it sticks its head into the air pocket and begins to use its lungs. About a day later it begins regular breathing.

The chick has a special sharp point, called the *egg tooth*, at the tip of its beak. With this point the chick pecks the shell many, many times before it finally breaks through.

Once the chick has cracked a hole through the shell, it rests. The little open window lets it get used to the outside air. When the chick has rested, it may take several hours more for it to break the rest of the shell away and climb out.

Did you like this story? Read "Biggest Family" under Babies *in* Volume 2.

Ancient Egypt

Giant, fierce-looking statues guard this lonely desert, where long ago one of the greatest kingdoms thrived—the kingdom of ancient Egypt. The statues are so huge that even the largest of all deserts, the Sahara Desert, can't hide them.

Behind the statues, strange pointed buildings as tall as skyscrapers reach toward the cloudless sky.

Nearby are broken columns of stone so huge that a hundred men could stand on top of them. The first log cabin was built in America more than 300 years ago, but these enormous creations have towered over the hot desert more than ten times that long.

For thousands of years, travelers have come from many lands to gaze at these sights and wonder what kind of giants made these things and what happened to those mighty people.

For a very, very long time ancient Egypt remained a land of mystery. The story of the Egyptians was painted in bright colors on Egyptian monuments, but it was painted in a strange picture writing called *hieroglyphics*, which no one could understand.

Then one day a flat stone was discovered that had some hieroglyphics on it as well as some writing in a language that people knew—Greek. Scholars thought that maybe the same story was written in both languages. By studying the two, the scholars learned to read the picture language.

The things they learned helped them know more about the ancient kings called *pharaohs*, after whom the statues were modeled. The pharaohs weren't really giants, but the Egyptians made the statues large so that everyone would see how powerful and godlike their pharaohs were. The strange pointed buildings, called *pyramids*, were built for the pharaohs, too.

The ancient Egyptians believed that when their pharaoh died, he joined the gods, and that on his journey to the gods he would want all the things that he had enjoyed on Earth.

A pyramid was built to hold all of the pharaoh's fine things. Each pharaoh needed many, many rooms to hold all of his riches. The rooms in the pyramids were filled with gold and silver, precious jewels, royal robes, golden furniture, gleaming boats and chariots, and weapons.

The pharaoh's body was wrapped in many layers of linen. The people thought that this would protect the dead pharaoh on his journey to the gods. The body wrapped in linen, called a *mummy,* was placed inside a beautiful case decorated with gold, silver, and jewels.

Each pharaoh wanted his pyramid to be bigger than all the others. Everyone had to help. Boatmen brought huge stones down the long Nile River. It took many years to cut and move all the thousands and sometimes millions of stones and to place them one on top of the other. Many thousands of slaves toiled all their lives to do it.

Other men made the golden furniture or painted pictures on the walls. Almost all of Egypt's riches were carried into the pyramids.

Afterward, each room was sealed with enormous stones and the entrance carefully sealed and hidden.

But after many years, despite everything, robbers broke into almost all of the rooms and took the gold and other precious things. It was a great crime to steal from the pyramids, but it was also wrong for the pharaohs to have the beautiful things buried where no one could use or enjoy them.

Some of the treasures of ancient Egypt have been found and can be seen today in museums. But only the crumbling statues and empty pyramids remain to point out where one of the greatest kingdoms once stood.

Black Pharaohs of Ancient Egypt

At any moment now these soldiers will race across the field and attack their enemy. They stand waiting for the signal to charge. Who do you think will give the signal?

Most people would say the leader. The leader of this army is Piankhi, the big man in front with his arm raised. (Piankhi was a great *pharaoh*, or king, of Egypt.) But Piankhi is not the one who will give the signal for the fighting to begin. . . .

Piankhi's army was so powerful that many cities up and down the long Nile River threw open their gates so that this mighty army could enter without fighting. When an enemy did decide to fight, a strange thing happened. It was important to Piankhi—and to his god Amon—that he always be a fair leader. Piankhi would never let his army swoop down on an enemy until the enemy was ready. He let the enemy give the signal for the attack.

All of this was so long ago that it is hard for us to find out very much about it today. But although Piankhi and other pharaohs lived before there were any cameras, we do know something of what the pharaohs were like. One visitor, a Greek historian named Herodotus, wrote that the Egyptians were "black and curly haired." Other writers of history tell about Egyptians whose skins were bronze or copper colored.

We can see ancient Egyptian statues carved in rock. And we can study paintings of the pharaohs, which show their skins as being bronze or copper colored, dark tan, yellow brown, or black. When drawing a person, the Egyptians used white paint only if the person was a visitor from a distant land or a white slave who had been sent to the pharaoh as a gift from another ruler.

Piankhi was only one of many pharaohs to rule ancient Egypt.

Taharqa, another pharaoh of Egypt, worked to make life more comfortable and enjoyable for his people. He wanted them to have the food and clothing and houses that they needed. But Taharqa knew that other things were important, too, and so he encouraged people to enjoy paintings and songs. Taharqa also was a powerful warrior who won many battles. He was ruler over a large land—a land so large that he called himself "Emperor of the World."

Not all the pharaohs, whether black skinned or bronze, were powerful warriors. Tutankhamen was very young when he became pharaoh. He wasn't even so big or so strong as many others his age. But he was not at all surprised to find himself pharaoh of Egypt. His father-in-law, Ikhnaton, had been pharaoh before him, and sometimes, when a pharaoh had no sons of his own, the royal crown was handed on to a pharaoh's son-in-law.

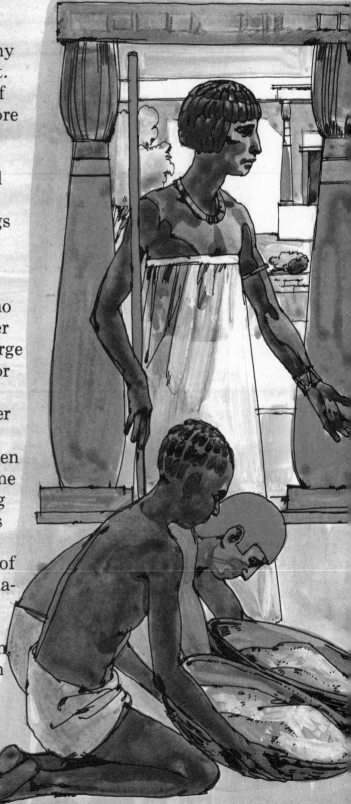

Royal artists carved a picture of Tutankhamen and his wife, Ankhesenpaaton, on the back of the pharaoh's throne. The picture was covered with gold and decorated with colored ceramic figures. It was made thousands of years ago. But today it shows us what Tutankhamen and many of the great pharaohs were like.

You may also read about ancient Greece under Greeks *in Volume 7.*

Down the River to Cairo

Abbas woke up early on this special morning. Today he was leaving for Cairo. He was one of three in his class at school who had been chosen to take part in the gymnastic celebration on his country's Independence Day.

Abbas lived in Egypt, in northern Africa. The town where he lived was Aswan, on the Nile River. The Nile is the longest river in the world, and today Abbas was going to sail down the river on a boat. He was sailing all the way to the big city of Cairo, many days to the north, near where the Nile empties into the sea.

Abbas gulped down his breakfast. His mother had already gone to the river to do the laundry, but she had left him his breakfast of beans, cheese made from water buffalo's milk, and dark bread.

When Abbas reached the river, he found his mother waiting beside a *felucca*, an Egyptian sailboat used for traveling from village to village along the Nile. Abbas' teacher and classmates were already on the boat. Abbas hugged his mother and hurried on board. He waved and watched the water widen as the boat moved slowly away from the shore.

The water was gray blue and the land was green, but Abbas knew that the green did not reach many miles beyond the river's edge. Most of Egypt was dry, brown desert country. Before his family had moved to Aswan, they had lived on a small farm on the edge of the desert. Abbas had never gone to school there because his father had needed him on the farm, where they had tried to grow as much rice and corn and fruit as possible. It had never been quite enough. Abbas had always been a little bit hungry. Now his father worked on the famous Aswan High Dam on the Nile River, and Abbas went to school.

The Aswan High Dam was enormous. The water that the dam held back was used to irrigate growing crops so that people in this poor country would have enough to eat.

In school Abbas had studied about Cairo. There, instead of using camels to pull carts to market, people had trucks and automobiles. And some people wore the kind of clothes that were worn in Europe and America. Both Abbas and his father wore a *galabia,* a kind of long shirt. When they worked outside under the hot sun, this garment kept them cool. And at night when it got cold, it kept them warm. On his head Abbas' father wore a *fez*, a tight-fitting red cap with a tassel on it.

Abbas knew that electricity was used to light the houses and streets of Cairo. On the farm, there had been no electricity for lights or stoves or anything else. They had used the dried bush of cotton plants as fuel for cooking because there was little wood near the desert. In Aswan, the house where Abbas lived was made of sunbaked mud and straw, with a roof of cornstalks

61

or palm branches. About the only thing that Abbas expected might be the same in Cairo was the police. They were everywhere in Egypt, telling people what to do and what not to do.

Suddenly Abbas stood very still, listening hard. From across the water he heard the faint cry of a *muezzin*—a crier—on top of a *mosque*—a Muslim church. The muezzin was calling the Muslims to prayer. Like most Egyptians, Abbas was a Muslim. Five times a day he knelt in the direction of Mecca, the holy city, and bowed his head in prayer.

Abbas' father had taken a trip to Mecca, as all Muslims hope to do. When he returned, he painted words above the door on the outside of his house to let everyone know that he had seen the holy city.

Abbas looked at the sun to determine which way to face when he knelt to pray. The sun was hot. The water, nearly blue here in the middle of the wide river, looked cool. The boat was not sailing fast. Abbas thought how nice it would be to have a swim. He heard a splash at the side of the boat and saw an enormous crocodile with the same idea.

Abbas knelt quickly and bowed to Allah, the Muslim God. He wished that when he returned home, his father would let him write on the outside of their house. He would like to tell everyone of the wonders that he knew he was going to see in Cairo.

There are other stories about Africa *in Volume 1.*

Cairo

EGYPT

Nile River

Aswan

Where Am I?

The people were angry. They were ashamed. That terrible Mr. Eiffel was ruining their beautiful city.

Many visitors were coming to see the World's Fair. But now all they would see was Mr. Eiffel's ugly pile of iron scraps. It would be so high they couldn't miss it. It was going to be the tallest building in the world!

Mr. Eiffel told them that his building would be beautiful when it was finished. He told them they would love it, and that the visitors would, too. But the people said they could not love anything *that* ugly.

Finally the day came. The building was finished. At least, Mr. Eiffel *said* it was finished. But how could a building be finished when there were strips of iron with spaces between them that you could see through? That wind could blow through? That rain and snow could go through? What kind of building was this anyway? Hardly any windows. No walls of wood or brick or stone.

But there it was. And as the people looked, many of them changed their minds. They didn't think the building was ugly now. They thought it was beautiful. Sometimes it happens that way. People think they won't like something if it is different or new. But when they see it, they like it.

They liked Mr. Eiffel's building—a graceful tower of iron that stretched into the sky.

The Eiffel Tower is not the tallest building in the world today. But it still—100 years later—has a restaurant on top, where people can eat and see all over the city. I am there now with my father and my mother. We have come to visit this beautiful city of Paris.

Look under Where Am I? *in Volume 16 and find Eiffel Tower on the map.*

EINSTEIN, ALBERT

The Man Who Had the Answers

Albert found school very difficult. His teacher would tap her pointer against the blackboard impatiently while she waited for him to answer her questions. But Albert always had to think about many things before he could answer. After all, he would say to himself, there are many different things to think about before you can say *anything* is absolutely certain.

When his teacher wasn't asking Albert a question, Albert would think of a question to ask *her*. And often when he did, she would get red in the face and angry at Albert for thinking up questions she couldn't answer.

The more Albert learned, the more he found to think about. The more he thought about, the more questions he thought of to ask.

He knew that the Earth, other planets, the moon, and the sun are just a part of what we call the *universe*. He knew that the universe is also made up of all the stars we can see with our eyes and millions and millions more that we can see only with the largest telescopes and still more—we think—that are so far away that they can't be seen at all. And he also knew that all these stars and our own bodies and everything else are made up of atoms so tiny they can't be seen even with the best microscope.

He thought there must be some rules to explain why everything in the universe, big and little, acts as it does. Why don't the stars moving around in the sky bump into each other? What makes the tiny atoms stick together to form all the different things there are?

Albert Einstein thought and thought until he believed he had some of the answers. And then people started asking *him* questions because he had answers for many things that scientists had been trying to figure out for many, many years.

How to Pick a Leader

When a pack of wolves needs a leader, it has a simple way of getting one. The strongest wolves have a terrible fight, and the one who wins is the leader.

People have figured out a better way of choosing leaders. They hold *elections*.

This means that on a certain day people go to a special place called a *polling place*. There each person gets a piece of paper called a *ballot*. On the ballot are the names of the men and women who want to be chosen as leaders.

CANDIDATE BALLOT

○ REPUBLICAN   ○ DEMOCRATIC
FOR MAYOR   FOR MAYOR

☐ ALBERT DREW   ☐ JOHN COLMAN

FOR CITY CLERK   FOR CITY CLERK

☐ THOMAS CHAMBERS   ☐ JOSEPH FLYNN

FOR CITY TREASURER   FOR CITY TREASURER

☐ ROBERT MEYERS   ☐ DONALD TATE

FOR CITY COUNCILMAN   FOR CITY COUNCILMAN

☐ JACK SMITH   ☐ HOLLIS AILING

68

Each person goes into a *voting booth* and makes a mark beside the names of the people he wants as leaders. This is called *voting*. (In many places there are machines in the booths. People pull small levers next to the names, and each machine makes a record of their votes.)

In a voting booth, only the voter can see the names of the people he is voting for. No one can make him vote for anyone but his own choice. He votes a *secret ballot*.

After he votes—that is, after he marks his ballot—he takes the ballot outside the booth and puts it into the *ballot box*.

At the end of election day, the election judges count the ballots. The people who get the most votes win the election and become the leaders.

People in a *democracy* feel that leaders should be changed at regular times. That way, no one leader can become too strong, too important, or too bossy. In each election others are given a chance to become leaders and try out new ideas. The United States is a democracy.

70

Not everyone lives in a democracy. Some countries in the world are *dictatorships*. In a dictatorship one man or a small group of men run the country. Sometimes a man becomes a dictator because enough people want him to rule their country and give him the power to do it. A dictator does not have to ask people what they want him to do. He tells people what to do, and if they don't do it, he can put them in prison or even have them killed.

The president of a country is not the only one who is chosen in an election. In the United States, *governors*—the leaders of states—also are elected. So are the *mayors*—the leaders of some towns and cities. There may even be an election for a class leader or a church leader.

Voting in an election is a good way to pick a leader.

If you liked this story,
look up Leaders *in Volume 9.*

Electricity, Please

Peter entered the Pierce Hardware Store and held up his flashlight.

"Want to buy some electricity?" Mr. Pierce asked.

"Yes, if you mean electricity in batteries," Peter answered.

Mr. Pierce led the way to the counter where the batteries were kept.

"Let's see what size your flashlight takes," he said. "We've got all sizes."

Peter looked at all the different sized batteries. Some of them were very small. He stared at the automobile batteries.

"Automobiles must need more electricity than flashlights," said Peter, "because they're so big."

"That's right," Mr. Pierce agreed.

"Electricity makes the light to light my house at night," Peter said. "And it makes the heat in our electric stove."

"Houses don't use batteries," said Mr. Pierce. "The electricity for all the houses in a city comes from one special place—a place called a *power plant*, where they make electricity."

"How does the electricity get from the power plant to my house?"

"It goes through wires. Some of the wires are under the ground where you can't see them, and some are fastened on poles."

Mr. Pierce picked up two flashlight batteries and held out his hand for the flashlight. Peter handed it to him.

"Do my parents have to pay for the electricity the same as when I buy a flashlight battery?"

"That's right. There's a little box at your house called an *electric meter*. The electricity you use goes through the meter. In the meter there are little pointers that look like the hands on a clock."

"I've seen it," said Peter. "It's in our cellar, and it has a wheel that spins around."

73

"At suppertime in the winter," said Mr. Pierce, "when your mother is cooking, and the electric heater is going, and the television and lots of electric lights are on, the wheel spins very fast and the pointers turn.

"Every month or two the meter man comes to read the meter. Then the electric company knows how much electricity your family has used."

Mr. Pierce opened one end of Peter's flashlight. He took out the old batteries and put in the new ones.

"Thank you," said Peter. "How much do they cost?"

"Better try it first," said Mr. Pierce.

Peter snapped the flashlight button, but the flashlight still didn't work.

"Must be the bulb." Mr. Pierce opened the front end of the flashlight and took out the bulb. He held the bulb up so he could look at it.

"The filament is broken," he said.

"What's a *filament?*" asked Peter.

"The tiny wire inside the bulb," Mr. Pierce answered. "When the wire isn't broken the electricity goes through it. The wire gets very hot and it glows. The glow is the light we see."

Mr. Pierce put a new bulb in the flashlight. "When the wire is broken, the electricity can't go through, so the wire doesn't get hot and doesn't make any light," he added.

He handed the flashlight to Peter. This time Peter tried it and it worked.

"How much does the bulb cost?" asked Peter.

"Let's check the old batteries first," said Mr. Pierce. He took the new batteries out and put the old ones back in.

"Now try it," he said.

Peter snapped the button. This time the bulb glowed dimly.

"That's not bright enough," said Peter.

Mr. Pierce put the new batteries in the flashlight again. And then Peter paid him for the batteries and the bulb.

"Good-bye," said Peter, as he went out the door. "Thank you for the bulb and batteries—and the electricity."

There is a story under
Flashlight *in Volume 6,*
where you may find more facts
about electricity and how it works.

77

A Shocking Fish

Mari and Dot stood watching some very long, lazy-looking fish move slowly through the water. They were strange fish. Their tail parts seemed to take up most of their long bodies.

The girls were close enough to touch one. But they couldn't because there was a glass wall between them and the fish. Mari and Dot were in an *aquarium,* which is a place that might be called a zoo for fish. Instead of cages with bars, in an aquarium there are glass tanks full of water.

An attendant—a man who takes care of the aquarium—moved close. "That's a funny-looking fish, isn't it? It really *is* a fish, though. It's called an *electric eel."*

"Electric?" Mari said. "Is there really electricity in it?"

"There is so much electricity in it," the attendant said, "that if it touched you it could shock you hard enough to knock you down. A big one might even knock down a horse!"

"Wow! How does the electricity get inside the fish?"

"The fish makes its own electricity. Some of the muscles in its long tail are like batteries."

"Could its electricity work our electric toaster?" Dot asked.

"No, its electric charges come and go too quickly. But it could light a neon lamp. A neon lamp needs only a short charge of electricity."

Dot shivered. "Doesn't the electricity hurt the eel?"

"No," the attendant told her, "and it won't hurt other electric eels, either. But when an eel comes close to a fish that it wants to eat, it gives the fish an electric shock so it can't move. Then it's easy for the eel to catch the fish. Electric eels swallow their food whole because they have no teeth. They have no scales either. How would you like one for a pet?"

Dot shivered again. "I wouldn't," she said. "Not even a little one."

More About Electricity

You can't see electricity, but you know it's there when you see an electric light go on or hear the telephone ring or see an electric eggbeater whirling. And you know it's there when you get an electric shock! You feel it, and it doesn't feel good.

Getting a shock from an electric socket in your house can be very dangerous. That's why you should never play with the sockets or the wires that go into them. If you do, you can be hurt or even killed.

Electricity comes into your house through thick underground wires called *cables*. It moves along wires in the walls to the sockets and from them along the wires that go to the telephone, the lamp, the eggbeater. . . .

Electricity moves easily along things that are made of silver, copper, or iron. That's why copper wires are used to carry the electricity that makes the lights shine, the telephone work, the eggbeater whirl. . . .

Electricity doesn't pass through rubber, plastic, wood, or cloth. That's why wires carrying electricity are usually coated with rubber or plastic. This keeps the electricity from getting away and being wasted or starting a fire or shocking someone.

If a wire coated with plastic or rubber is wound around and around, it makes a *coil*. If electricity is sent along the coil that is wrapped around a piece of iron, something surprising happens. The iron becomes a magnet and will attract things made of iron and steel. Such a magnet is called an *electromagnet*.

As soon as the electricity is turned off, the electromagnet isn't a magnet anymore. If the magnet is holding something when the electricity is turned off, the magnet drops it.

When huge piles of scrap iron need to be moved, a very powerful, round electromagnet swung by a crane is used.

The crane operator places the electromagnet on a pile and then turns on the electricity. Now, when he lifts the electromagnet, much of the scrap is held by the magnet. The operator swings the electromagnet around until it is over the freight car being loaded. Now he turns off the electricity. The scrap drops into the freight car, and the crane operator swings the electromagnet back to the scrap pile to get more.

A Special School

In the country of Burma in Asia there are many little one-room schoolhouses. They hold only one pupil at a time.

On the first day of school a wrinkled old teacher stands at the gate waiting for the pupil to arrive.

The pupil is only five years old. He is brought to school by teen-age boys. But he doesn't go in at once.

He is not sure he wants an education.

The teacher helps him make up his mind by shoving him into the schoolhouse from behind. Then the boys close the gate.

Now the pupil is sure he doesn't want an education! He starts to howl.

The boys gather around, offering him bananas and sweets. The pupil is very fond of eating, so he stops howling now and then to take a banana. Finally, after many bananas, he decides that school isn't so bad. Perhaps he will stay.

What kind of school is this?

It is a school for little Indian elephants. The wrinkled, old teacher is a wrinkled old elephant about 50 years old called a *koonkie*. The boys or men who help to train the little elephant are elephant riders. They are called *oozies*.

One oozie will become the little elephant's own driver and will stay with him all his life if he can.

What does the little elephant learn in school?

After a great deal of fussing around, and after pounds and pounds of bananas, he learns to let the oozie sit on his head. He learns the meaning of a few words, such as "Sit down!" and "Stand up!" But mostly he learns touch signals. If the oozie touches him on the ear or leans forward or backward, the elephant knows he is to go faster or slower or to stop or to kneel.

If the elephant is trained with kindness and patience, if he is praised and fussed over and given many treats, he will learn quickly. When he is older, he will work in a forest, dragging heavy logs or pulling up trees.

There are two kinds of elephants, Indian and African. Indian elephants are somewhat smaller than the African, and because they are gentler, many of them are trained to work for man. Most of the elephants we see in zoos or doing tricks in circuses are Indian.

Wild elephants live in herds in the forests of southeastern Asia. They are fairly easy to capture.

First, men build a strong pen.

Then some men called *beaters*, carrying drums and horns and clappers and gongs, get behind a herd of elephants. They make such a racket beating their drums and gongs that they scare and confuse the elephants. The elephants run away from the noise and right into the pen.

Of course, they don't like it at first. But if they are treated kindly, in time they are willing to learn, just as the little elephant was.

African elephants are larger and stronger than the Indian elephants. They have bigger ears and thicker skin. They get to be more than 11 feet tall—about twice as tall as a man. They weigh more than 12,000 pounds—as much as a school bus weighs! They are the largest animals that walk on land—the only animals in the world that are larger are whales.

Elephants used to live in many places in Africa, but so many were killed by hunters for their valuable ivory tusks that there are not so many left anymore.

Male elephants have huge tusks from six to nine feet long. They use them for digging up roots to eat and for carrying things and, if necessary, for fighting.

But elephants don't fight much. Except for man, they have no enemies. They are so big that no other animals attack them. And they don't attack or eat other animals.

They eat leaves and bark and fruits and nuts and vegetables.

They travel in herds, following a leader, and are always looking for a good place to have a picnic. When they find a nice little grove of trees, they have dinner. They break the branches off the trees to eat the leaves as we would break off a stalk of celery. Sometimes they just butt with their heads and knock down a whole tree.

85

Baby elephants shuffle along with a traveling herd, hanging onto their mothers' tails with their trunks. The mothers take good care of their babies. Sometimes they even "plaster" them with mud. Does a mother elephant know that this gives her baby some protection against insect bites and stings? It seems so. All the elephants keep an eye on the babies, for they are the pets of the herd.

If an elephant happens to be sick or hurt, the other elephants take care of it, too. They never go on and leave it behind.

Elephants don't like the heat, and during the hot part of the day, they might take a nap. The older elephants sleep standing up, but the babies lie down and stretch out.

Elephants like to swim. When they come to a river, they wade in to cool off. They splash and squirt each other and give each other showers. On their backs, the babies sometimes slide down mudbanks. They all have a wonderful time.

A very special thing about an elephant is its trunk.

It's about six feet long and made up of strong, easily bending muscles.

The elephant breathes through its trunk and smells with it, so it is something like a nose.

He picks up food and heavy weights with it, so it is something like an arm.

He picks up tiny nuts and blades of grass with it, so it is something like a hand.

He makes loud noises with it, so it is something like a horn.

He sucks water up in it and gives himself a shower, so it is something like a garden hose.

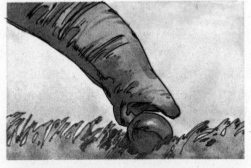

When he swims underwater, he sticks it up in the air like a snorkel and breathes through it.

Mother elephants stroke and cuddle their babies with it.

And elephant sweethearts link trunks and walk off into the forest together.

The Little People

Susan had discovered the magical world of fairyland. Tonight her mother was telling the story about the poor shoemaker. Susan sat in her mother's lap, her feet in her worn canvas sneakers twisting as she listened with delight.

"The poor shoemaker worked very hard," Susan's mother said, "but he couldn't make shoes fast enough. Often he and his wife and their ten children were hungry.

"But one morning when the poor shoemaker woke up, he rubbed his eyes in great surprise. There on his workbench were six pairs of shiny new shoes that had not been there when he went to bed. In great joy he sold the shoes and bought leather to make some more. When he woke up the next morning . . . guess what?"

"I know," Susan said, "the same thing as before. The leather was all sewn and nailed and made into new shoes."

"Yes. And this happened every night. People bought the shoes, and soon the poor shoemaker was not poor any longer. He had all the money he needed to buy food and clothing for his family, and pretty toys for his children.

"Then one night the shoemaker and his wife decided to stay up and see who it was that made these wonderful shoes. They could hardly believe what they saw!"

"I know," Susan said, "I know. It was the *elves* who came and made the shoes."

"Yes," Susan's mother said, "the tiny, tiny elves came and sewed and rapped and tapped and polished . . . and ran away at dawn when the shoes were finished."

Susan twisted herself right off her mother's lap. "What wonderful little people! Are elves real? Really real?"

"What do you think?" her mother asked.

"I don't think so—not really. But I wish they were."

"Well, if you wish it hard enough," her mother said, "that makes them *almost* real, don't you think?"

"Oh yes!" Susan said. She looked down at her old sneakers. One of them had a hole in the toe. She wiggled her toe and laughed.

"Maybe if I left my sneakers by my bed tonight, the elves might come and make them new again."

Her mother smiled. "Why don't you try it and see?"

"I shall," Susan said.

She had hardly gone to sleep when she heard a voice calling, "Susan." It was a tiny whisper of a voice, almost like faraway music.

She opened her eyes, and there on her pillow was a tiny elf wearing a green suit, high-heeled leather boots, and a bright red hat with a feather in it.

He was motioning to her. "Come on," he said.

"Come on where?" she asked.

"To fairyland. All you have to do is get up and close your eyes and turn around three times."

She did as the elf said, and when she opened her eyes, she was in a beautiful forest with thousands of fireflies lighting her way.

"Welcome to fairyland, Susan. I am the elf king."

Turning around at the unexpected voice, Susan was surprised to find someone as tall as she was.

"I thought elves were supposed to be smaller than people," she said.

The elf king laughed. "We're not the same size as you," he explained. "You've become the same size as we are. We'll change you back again, don't worry."

He took her by the hand, and away they went through the air. "May Eve is the only night we have visitors in fairyland," he said, "and you have been especially chosen."

"There are so many questions I want to ask," Susan said. "First, how old are you?"

"Old as the winds and the rain," the elf king said, with a wink. "And as old as the night and the day."

"What do you mean by that?"

"A long time ago, when people didn't know how to explain the sun and the moon, the winds and the rain, the thunder and the lightning, they had to make up stories to explain them. So they made up the little people. Stories were told about the magical little people, and soon nearly everyone believed in them because there seemed to be no other explanation for many things that happened. We were praised for everything good that happened and blamed for everything bad. But when scientists discovered *why* there was day and night, *why* there was wind and rain, and *why* there was thunder and lightning, people stopped believing in us. But some men who loved children wrote about us. Some of the best writers were the Grimm brothers, Perrault, and Hans Christian Andersen."

"Where is fairyland?" Susan asked.

"Wherever you want it to be," said the elf king. "In your dreams. Under a fairy hill. In the forest. On an invisible island. In a flower. But it's not on a map."

"I know there are different kinds of little people——"

"Sure. Look down there. Those are trooping fairies. They are very fond of music and dancing. They make their homes high in the treetops."

"Where do those elves dressed all in green come from?"

"They're from England and Scotland. And the ones with the red hats are leprechauns from Ireland."

"Is that a fairy or an elf sitting in the buttercup?"

"That's one of the elf gardeners. It's his job to take care of the flowers. Most elves and fairies have special jobs to do. Some spin clothes. The water fairies are weavers. Some find lost children. Others help Santa make toys. And some, as you know, are very good shoemakers."

"Oh-oo-oo!" cried Susan. "What's that? It's flying around my head."

"That's a pixie. Pixies love to play tricks on people. They ride through the air on grass stalks or dandelion fluff. Pixies have a special dust to change themselves into moths, to make things disappear and reappear, and to grant wishes."

"Can you grant wishes?" asked Susan.

The elf king nodded. "Yes," he said. "Most of us can."

"What kind of fairies are those—the ones dressed in brown rags?"

"Those are the brownies. They belong to the family of helping fairies. They help around the house at night by tidying up the kitchen, cleaning pots and pans, or sewing. But, don't give them clothes for a present, or they'll never come back. A bowl of milk is all they want."

Susan yawned. The sun was beginning to come up, so the elf king said that it was time to get home. Susan watched the little people join hands and dance in a circle. Faster and faster they whirled until just watching them made her dizzy, and she fell asleep.

When she woke up in the morning, she saw her mother standing near, smiling down.

"Oh, Mom," she said. "I had the most wonderful dream." She stopped because by this time she was sitting up and looking at the place where she had left her sneakers before going to bed. "Mom, look!" she said. "Look! The elf shoemakers made my old sneakers new again!"

Her mother just smiled, and Susan said, "You and Dad bought them for me, didn't you?"

"I'm not telling," her mother said.

Susan slipped her bare feet into the new sneakers. She grinned. "They feel like fairy slippers. I think I could *almost* fly with them."

The Big Country on the Little Islands

Johnny Atkins looked forward to the month of August. That was when many visitors came to his village of Burford in the Cotswold Hills of England. Things here had changed little for hundreds of years. The houses were made of stone. Some of the roofs were thatched with straw. Everywhere there were lovely gardens of hollyhocks and deep red roses.

Johnny's parents owned the Crown and Thistle Inn. Every room was rented in August. The tourists told Johnny that the Cotswold country was the most beautiful in all England. Johnny was polite and thanked them, but he wanted to find out for himself. He wanted to see more of England.

One day Mr. Carson, an old army friend of his father's, arrived. He had come all the way from Australia with his wife and his son Bruce to show them England. Bruce and Johnny liked each other right away. When the Carsons asked Johnny to go with them, both boys were very happy.

Their first stop was London, one of the largest cities in the world. They entered the city by the Great West Road. The streets were full of shiny automobiles and red double-deck buses, and the Carson family and Johnny drove on slowly past Buckingham Palace, the London home of the kings and queens of England. Now Queen Elizabeth II and her family live there. The queen's personal standard, or flag, was flying on the roof of the palace. That meant she was at home. When she is away from London, the flag is taken down.

The traffic got heavier and the crowds got larger as the street curved and became a great circle.

"This is Piccadilly Circus," said Mr. Carson.

Bruce and Johnny said they couldn't see any circus. Mr. Carson laughed and said that *circus* is an old word for circle. The street and sidewalk went around the statue of a boy. Here there were people from almost every country in the world. Mrs. Carson looked hard at the people and the confusion and said the place looked like a circus to her.

95

In a neighborhood of London called Westminster, they saw a large church. It was Westminster Abbey, where for 900 years all but two of the English kings and queens have been crowned.

Near the abbey was a huge gray stone building with a large clock tower. Suddenly a deep bell went *bong!*

"Listen!" cried Johnny. "That's Big Ben! Big Ben is the name of the clock bell."

Bruce said, "Oh, everybody in Australia knows that."

Mr. Carson said that the building was the Palace of Westminster, where the Houses of Parliament met.

"We have a Parliament in Australia, too," said Bruce. "That's where the government makes laws."

"The United States has a kind of Parliament," said Mrs. Carson. "But it is called Congress."

The Carsons and Johnny boarded a little boat and sailed down the river Thames, which flows right through the city. The docks and piers of the Port of London stretched far down the river. There was much excitement and activity. Food from all parts of the world was being taken off some of the big ships, and manufactured goods were being put on others.

Johnny had heard about the white cliffs of Dover. He was very happy when the Carsons said that they, too, wanted to see them. To reach Dover, they drove through the quiet green countryside of Kent. They saw some hop fields. Hops are used in making beer and some medicines. Scattered throughout the fields were the little round brick houses with pointed roofs in which the hops are stored and dried.

From Dover it is only 21 miles across the English Channel to the coast of France. Some very good swimmers have swum the Channel at this point.

The Carsons and Johnny discovered that the cliffs of Dover really *are* white. They are made of chalk and stretch for miles along the coast. In olden days these high cliffs discouraged enemies from attacking England.

That evening Mr. Carson said that tomorrow they would take a train from one end of England to the other.

He told them they were also going to Scotland, Northern Ireland, and Wales. These countries, together with England, are known as the United Kingdom.

97

On the train next morning, Mr. Carson pointed out the woods near the town of Nottingham, north of London. "That used to be part of Sherwood Forest," he said.

Both boys looked quickly. They knew that many years ago Sherwood Forest had been the home of Robin Hood.

As the train went northward, it ran through a part of the country where there were factory cities, such as Sheffield and Leeds. Here the boys saw forests of tall smokestacks.

Then the land began to get hilly. The towns grew smaller and farther apart. The air was cooler. Finally, with a clatter, the train crossed a bridge over the river Tweed into Scotland. Purple heather bloomed on the hillsides. The boys could see shepherds watching their sheep. Soon the train pulled into the station at Edinburgh, the capital of Scotland. Of all the historic sights they saw in Edinburgh, Johnny and Bruce liked best the castle up on the hill, in the center of the city.

From Scotland the Carsons and Johnny flew in a plane across the North Channel to Northern Ireland. Ireland is called the Emerald Isle because it is so green. The air is mild, the rain falls often, and nowhere in the world is there a more restful and green countryside.

Ireland is supposed to be the home of *leprechauns*—tiny, cranky old men who make shoes for the fairies.

Johnny and Bruce looked hard for leprechauns.

"Maybe," said Bruce, "only Irishmen can see them."

They flew back toward England across the Irish Sea but stopped first in Wales, a mountainous country not far from Johnny's home. Because much of Wales is too steep and rocky to be plowed, sheep are raised and allowed to graze on the mountain slopes. Coal mining is also important.

On the train going back to Johnny's village, Johnny and Bruce tried to learn a few Welsh words. But it was just too difficult.

"Don't feel bad, lads," said one Welshman. "Look at the name of the village we are passing through. It's supposed to be the longest name in the world."

The boys looked and saw LLANFAIRPWLLGWYNGYLLGOGERYCHWYRNDROB-WLL-LLANTYSILIOGOGOGOCH

When they got back to Burford, Johnny said good-bye to his good friends the Carsons. They promised to visit him again. Johnny realized now that his town and his hills were as beautiful as any others to be found in the United Kingdom.

If you liked this story, look under Buckingham Palace *in Volume 2 and* London *in Volume 9. You may read about* Robin Hood *in Volume 13.*

More About England

ENGLAND

London

England, a small country about as big as the state of Alabama, was once the most powerful country in the world.

England covers more than half of a rocky island that lies off the coast of continental Europe. England, Wales, Scotland, and Northern Ireland together are known as the United Kingdom of Great Britain and Northern Ireland. Without Northern Ireland, they are called Great Britain. Some people say the British Isles or just Britain.

The rocky coasts of Britain have protected it from attack. It has been nearly 1,000 years since enemy soldiers landed there.

Because they lived on an island, the English people had to travel first by boat whenever they wanted to go anywhere outside their own country. The English people have been good sailors for a very long time—since the days when they first built their own ships and sailed all over the world.

England also built the greatest empire the world has ever known. In the late 1800s England ruled nearly one-fourth of the world's land area and one-fifth of its people. It ruled large parts of Asia, Africa, and North America. It ruled Australia, New Zealand, Canada, and most of India. It ruled places in South and Central America—and more than 1,000 islands.

England became very rich from its trade with the empire countries. English ships brought home products and materials from these countries and carried back things made in English factories.

But one day the people in the American colonies decided they wanted to run their own government and did not want to pay taxes any longer to England. So they rebelled and finally won their freedom. Since then other empire countries have also become free and independent.

As these countries became free, most of them wanted to stay friends with England. So they formed a kind of huge club called the Commonwealth of Nations. Each nation in the Commonwealth is free to rule itself, but the heads of these nations meet with the queen and prime minister in London about once a year. There they talk over their problems and try to advise and help each other.

Many of the world's finest writers, artists, and scientists are British. There are also many businessmen in Britain, which is one of the greatest manufacturing countries in the world. Much iron and coal are mined there. Steel is made there. And shipbuilding is a big business.

In 1956 Britain opened the world's first large-scale nuclear power station. It was the first country to make large amounts of electricity from nuclear energy.

To many people the British seem to be reserved at first—that is, they do not tell much about themselves until they know a person very well. They change their habits slowly. They don't like to change things just to be changing.

Many English people like tea in the morning. They also like tea with sandwiches and cakes in the afternoon. After dinner they may raise their glasses and drink a toast to the queen's health. Some Englishmen like to spend time in their clubs, where they play cards, read newspapers, and sometimes have lunch or dinner. There are men's clubs like this throughout England. There are also *pubs* —neighborhood places where people go to drink beer, meet other people, have friendly talks, and play darts.

English people like to walk, even in the rain. Many don't like furnace heat in their homes. They find it too hot and dry. There are many English *accents*—the way words are pronounced—and they rarely change. One Englishman often can tell what neighborhood another lives in just by his accent.

In spite of all this, the English have introduced a lot of new things to the world. Their music and singing groups have changed the style of music in many countries. London is not only a center of government and business but also a center for new ways of thinking. The English love the old and familiar, but they are not afraid of the new.

101

Few Against Many

A first adventure with mathematics

In the days of knights, castles made it possible for a few warriors to hold off many enemies. Protected by high walls, a few men in a castle could match the strength of many.

But what do you think would happen if two brave warriors met face-to-face beyond the castle walls? Suppose that each man was as strong and as brave as the other.

Would it make a difference if one brave man had a friend to help him? Or if he carried a sharp sword?

Or had a horse to ride?

Or carried a shield with which to protect himself?

Would our brave men of equal strength *still* be equally matched?

102

A friend
to help

A sword
to draw

A horse
to ride

A shield
to raise

Now, what picture would you put in each frame below to keep our brave men equally matched?

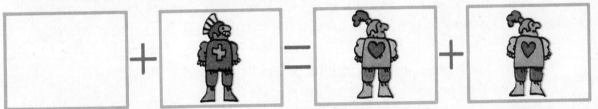

plus knight is the same as knight plus friend.

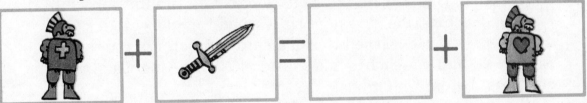

Knight plus sword is the same as   plus knight.

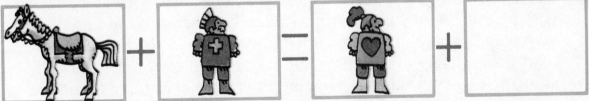

Horse plus knight is the same as knight plus

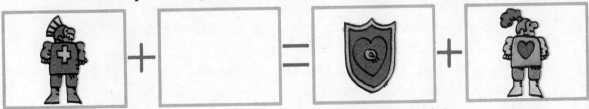

Knight plus   is the same as shield plus knight.

Other first adventures with mathematics may be found under Collections, Lines and Shapes. Measurement, Numbers, One-to-One, Plus and Minus, *and* Relationships.

Captain of the Dragon Ship

Leif Ericsson's people, the brave and fierce Vikings, loved adventure and danger. They sailed to far-off places—lands that none of them had ever seen before. Their ships were called *dragon ships*. They were long and low, with a tall mast and many strong oars for rowing when the wind stopped blowing. Carved at the front of each boat was the head of an ugly dragon or serpent, which was supposed to keep evil spirits away.

Leif grew up on the lonely, icy island of Greenland. There his adventurous father, Eric the Red, taught him to hunt for white foxes and sleek-skinned seals. Leif learned to fight with a sword and to wrestle. He learned to sail a ship through the roughest waters . . . and he reached the shores of North America almost 500 years before Columbus!

We don't know exactly how Leif's great discovery happened. There are many old stories about him and his crew. One story says that he lost his way in fog while sailing between Iceland and Greenland. Many days later, when the skies had cleared, he saw a new, mysterious shoreline. He and his crew anchored their dragon ship and explored this strange and different place. They found tall trees and grassy hills and fresh water. They saw so many tangled grapevines growing that Leif named the place Vinland. The men built huts and stayed through the snowy, cold winter.

The Vikings sailed to Vinland many times after that, until the Eskimos who lived there forced them to leave for good. For hundreds of years no one knew about Leif and his discovery. Scientists and explorers were never sure where he had landed or when.

Then, not many years ago, in a place now called Newfoundland, an explorer found some ruins, with parts of a stone house and a fireplace still standing. The house is thought to have been built about 1,000 years ago.

Leif Ericsson's house? We don't know for sure. But we do know that he was a brave captain who sailed unknown seas.

You may read about the Vikings in Volume 16.

The Boy Who Lives in a Snowhouse

The barking of the dogs awakened Akeeko, the Eskimo boy.

His mother was already up, making tea over the soft yellow flame that burned in the whale-oil lamp.

Akeeko slid from under the warm cover made of walrus skin and pulled on his trousers and his hooded fur jacket, or *parka*. Underneath all this he wore underwear made of skin from a caribou, with the warm fur turned toward his body. Over his boots he pulled on a pair of heavy outer boots. Last of all he put on his furry mittens.

Now he was ready to go out in the cold.

At the doorway to the snowhouse, or *igloo,* Akeeko lifted the curtain and crawled through the short snow tunnel that led outside.

There he saw his father and brothers harnessing the dogs to the sled. He laughed while he romped and tumbled in the snow with some of the young sled dogs.

Akeeko had lived all his life on the shores of the Arctic Ocean, about as close to the North Pole as people can live. Here in the middle of the summer the days are so long that the sun never stops shining. It stays light all night!

But this was winter, and in the winter there is a time when it stays dark all day, as well as all night, with only a little light sometimes from the moon.

Snug and warm under the round roofs of their snowhouses, the Eskimo families had lived through the dark days and nights. But now the frozen fish and meat were almost gone. It was time for the hunters to travel across the fields of snow and ice to look for food.

Their dogsled was loaded with bundles of animal skins to be used as night covers or windbreaks. The sled also carried knives, spears, bone fishhooks, and some frozen fish.

Akeeko watched closely until his father nodded and said, "Jump on, Little Seal. You are old enough now to go on your first hunting trip."

Akeeko rubbed his nose against his mother's nose (that's how Eskimos kiss) and waved good-bye. A long whip cracked. The dogs pushed against their harness and away they went, the sled runners making a singing sound on the cold, dry snow.

The air was cold, too—so cold that Akeeko kept his eyes nearly closed to keep them from freezing. But inside his fur clothes, Akeeko was not cold.

Akeeko's father was very wise about where to find hunting grounds. In the summer he went far inland from the sea, hunting for caribou on the great frozen plains, or *tundra*. Caribou are a kind of deer and travel in large herds. Some of the caribou meat was dried for use in the wintertime. The skin was made into clothes or stretched over driftwood poles to make summerhouses.

Today's hunt was a winter hunt, and instead of going inland, they went in the other direction, over the thick ice that covers much of the northern ocean. They were hunting for seals, and they hoped they might even find a walrus or a polar bear.

Akeeko's father drove the dogsled for many hours before he said, "We'll camp here."

Quickly, Akeeko's father and brothers took their knives and began to cut huge blocks of snow. With Akeeko helping, they piled up the snow blocks, and in an hour or two they had finished an igloo hunting lodge.

The hungry dogs had raw frozen fish for supper. They caught the fish in their opened mouths when Akeeko's father threw them, and they gulped the fish down in one big bite.

Akeeko and his hungry family had raw frozen fish, too, and a small piece of whale fat, or *blubber*. Blubber was almost like candy to Akeeko!

After supper the dogs dug holes for themselves in the snow and curled up and slept. Akeeko and his family, warm and snug, went to sleep in their igloo. Early in the morning they took their spears and axes and went hunting.

They found some air holes in the ice and sat for many hours hoping that a seal would poke its head above the water to breathe.

But no seals came. Akeeko was getting worried because when you get hungry in the far north, you can't just go to a store and buy something. The stores are far, far away. The only way to get something to eat is to go hunting.

Suddenly Akeeko heard one of his brothers shouting, "Seals! I have found seals! Come quickly."

With the others, Akeeko scrambled over giant cakes of ice piled up at the edge of a streak of water. When they reached a place where they could look down, they saw the seals. Many seals! They could spear a few and have enough food to last through the rest of the winter.

As Akeeko helped load the sled for the long journey home, he felt sad that his first hunting trip would soon be over.

But he felt happy, too!

There aren't very many Eskimos in the world. In all of Alaska and Canada, the giant island of Greenland, the other Arctic islands, and on the coast of northeast Asia, there are only about 50,000 Eskimos. That's no more than the number of people who might live in one small city in the United States.

Some Eskimos still live in the primitive way that Akeeko does. They buy almost nothing from stores. They use animal skins and bones, driftwood, and ivory from walrus tusks to make almost everything they need. They make their dogsleds, as well as special boats in which they paddle to hunt whales and other sea creatures. They get their food from land and sea and air.

But this way of life is changing for many Eskimos. People have been moving into the Eskimo country to dig mines, drill oil wells, and build airports and weather stations. Many of the Eskimos now live in or near these new towns. They trade in the stores, and their children go to school. They wear the same kind of clothes, eat the same kind of food, and work at the same jobs as we do.

Want to know more?
Read Greenland *in Volume 7 and* Winter *in Volume 16.*

Where Am I?

I am standing in the shadow of what must be the largest and strangest lion in the world. This lion is a statue. But many real lions *do* live in the wild places of this country. The people here honor the lion—just as people in some other countries honor the eagle. The ruler of this country is called "Lion of Judah."

Besides lions, many other animals live in the deserts and mountains of this country. There are elephants, leopards, hyenas, crocodiles, monkeys, gazelles—deerlike animals that leap high into the air—and *dik-diks*, which look like tiny deer not much higher than your knees. The birds include vultures, eagles, and fast-running ostriches.

The people have dark skin—black or brown or copper colored. They are friendly to visitors. They live in small villages in round mud houses with straw roofs. Most of them do some farming, and some are herdsmen with flocks of sheep, cows, or goats.

There aren't many big cities in this country. Because of the steep mountains and cliffs, it is hard to build railroads. But airplanes fly to the most settled parts. And where roads are too narrow and bumpy for cars and trucks, people use mules, donkeys, camels, or oxcarts.

At outdoor markets, things are sold on the ground. The people trade in salt, cloth, food, and live animals.

If you hear a buzzing sound, it probably comes from wild bees. People here eat much honey and make a drink from it, too. They also sell honey and beeswax to other countries.

But they sell more coffee than anything else. There are wild coffee trees and carefully tended coffee farms in Kaffa, a region in the southern part of the country. Some people say that Kaffa is where coffee was first used and that that is why coffee is called *coffee*—because it sounds like the name of the place where it was first used.

This is one of the oldest countries in the world. Its people have had to fight fiercely to stay free. The name of this country of the lions is Ethiopia.

Look under Where Am I? *in Volume 16 and find Ethiopia on the map.*

The Highest Climb

Each day the men climbed higher on the icy mountain cliffs. Finally, they reached a narrow shelf of rock, where most of the tired party stopped to rest. But two men continued to climb from this high camp.

The slippery rock made each step seem more difficult than the one before. In some places the two men had to cling to the steep rock like ants on a wall. The cold wind bit at their eyes and tugged at their clothes. It threatened to pull them loose from the mountain—to send them falling against the rock a thousand feet below.

The air was so thin that the two men had to breathe from tanks of oxygen strapped to their backs. They became so tired and cold that they could barely move.

They looked back down the icy slope . . . down . . . down to the black storm clouds. They were high above the clouds!

They started climbing toward the top again. Would they make it? Everyone who had tried before had failed. Many had been killed trying to climb to the windy, snow-covered top of this high mountain.

Slowly, steadily, they kept climbing until they reached the last icy cliff. They knew they were close to the top. But how close? Blinding, swirling snow kept them from seeing.

They kept climbing anyway. They had to chop places in the ice for their hands and feet. They kept on, blindly, until finally when they reached to feel the rock ahead, there was no rock. They knew then that they had reached the top.

It was on May 29, 1953, that Edmund Hillary and Tenzing Norgay reached the top of Mount Everest, the highest mountain in the world. They were the first men ever to do this. Mount Everest is in the Himalayan Mountains between India and China.

Where Am I?

This strange marshland is dark and hot—sometimes beautiful and sometimes dangerous. Wild animals hiss and wail in the muddy swamps. To travel here, you must ride in a boat. The waterways are shallow and clogged with growing plants, and they go in every direction. Unless you're used to them, the tree-buried waterways all look the same. You could get lost in a minute!

Boatmen move slowly and steer carefully so that their boats won't get stuck in the tough saw grass growing on the slippery banks. The roots of giant swamp trees—mangrove and cypress—rise up as if they were climbing right out of the water.

A mother alligator lies quietly in the thick mud. But she isn't sleeping. She's guarding her eggs, buried under a mound of sun-heated mud and old leaves. What seems to be a floating log *may* be a hungry alligator hunting for food.

The air is thick and heavy with dampness. Insects hum and buzz. The green forests are crowded with tangled vines. Some trees are dressed in ferns on which orchid flowers are growing. Tree snakes coil around hidden branches. Under some trees it's as dark as night even when the sun shines.

Tall, stick-legged birds with lacy plumes—egrets and spoonbills—wade in shallow pools. Gentle sea cows—manatees—swim through the muddy water, nibbling on water plants.

All these plants and animals live in Everglades National Park, part of a huge marsh in Florida called the Everglades—a swampland so large and so wild that parts of it never have been explored.

Look under Where Am I? *in Volume 16 and find the Everglades on the map.*

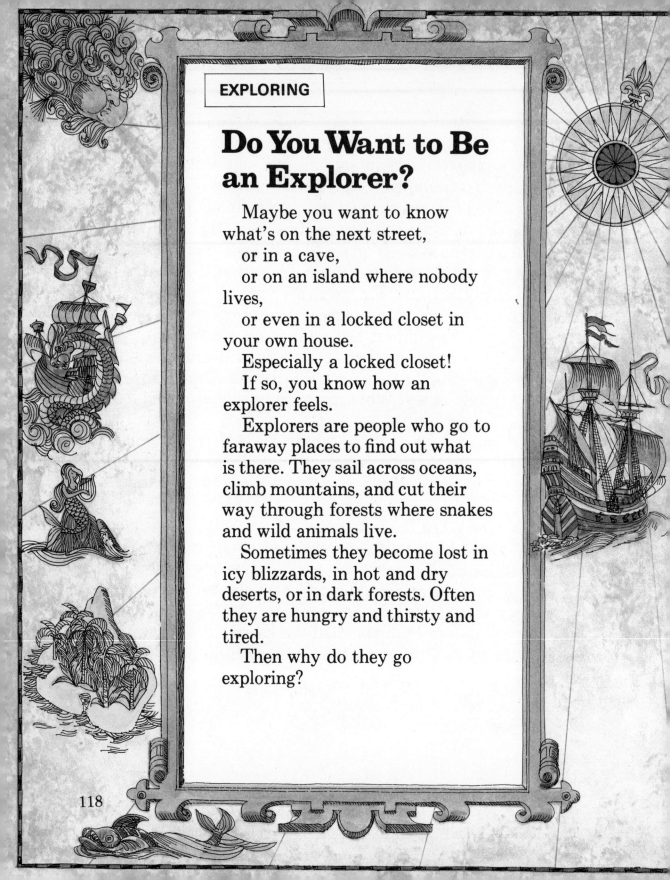

Do You Want to Be an Explorer?

Maybe you want to know what's on the next street,

or in a cave,

or on an island where nobody lives,

or even in a locked closet in your own house.

Especially a locked closet!

If so, you know how an explorer feels.

Explorers are people who go to faraway places to find out what is there. They sail across oceans, climb mountains, and cut their way through forests where snakes and wild animals live.

Sometimes they become lost in icy blizzards, in hot and dry deserts, or in dark forests. Often they are hungry and thirsty and tired.

Then why do they go exploring?

Long ago—very, very long ago —when there were no machines in the world and everybody lived in trees or caves, people went exploring to find food and water.

After people learned how to build houses, they went exploring for other reasons, too. Some went to look for gold and jewels and furs and spices. Some went to find new lands for their king or queen. Some went to find slaves to do their work for them. Some tried to find a new way to get to the other side of the world.

Perhaps the best reason of all for people to go exploring is that they are curious and want to go somewhere new. Many men have wanted to know what it was like in some faraway place.

112

An explorer named Ferdinand Magellan and his sailors left Spain and sailed toward the setting sun to see how far they could go. After sailing week after week on the ocean, they ran out of food. They became so hungry that they ate sawdust and leather.

One of the sailors told of "great and awful things of the ocean"—ugly flying fish, sharks, sea lions, giant crabs, and fearful sea serpents.

Finally, they sighted an unknown land. Their ships sailed through a narrow path, or *channel,* of stormy water between high mountains and came to another ocean—the biggest ocean in the world. Magellan named it the Pacific Ocean, and the channel where his ships sailed was named the Strait of Magellan.

One of Magellan's ships was the first to sail all the way around the world.

120

In the mountains of Mexico an
explorer named Cortés discovered
the land of the Aztec Indians. It
was like discovering a new world.
Some of the Aztec houses were
on floating islands in a lake.
Many houses were almost buried
in flowers.

Strange buildings—pyramids
made of stones—pointed high into the sky. Around the pyramids
for many miles was a tall new plant, green and waving in the wind.
Some of the explorers had never seen it before. They didn't know
what it was.

Corn! The tall, green, waving plant was corn.

The Aztecs also had gold—a lot of gold. The explorers knew
what that was. Some explorers were cruel and greedy people. They
fought the Indians and took their gold.

"I will find a way or make one," said Robert E. Peary.

Peary wanted to be first to reach the North Pole—a faraway place of ice and snow where it is light day and night in the middle of the summer and dark day and night in the middle of the winter.

Peary learned that explorers must be patient, as well as brave. He broke his leg and had to wait. He froze his toes and had to wait again. Storms and icy fog and polar bears caused more waiting. The sunlit snow almost blinded him. Some of his men died, and others turned back.

Only one man who had started out with him, Matthew Henson, was still with him when, finally, he reached the North Pole.

Look on the globe. You'll see
the South Pole, as well as the
North Pole. Both are places of
icy blizzards and are very cold.
With snowshoes and dog teams,
a man named Amundsen raced a
man named Scott to be the first
one to the South Pole. Amundsen
was first. Scott reached it soon
afterward, but he was so weak
from hunger and cold that he
died on the way home.

The first man to fly an airplane
over both the North Pole and
the South Pole was Admiral Byrd.

Today in an airplane an explorer can go farther in a minute
than a dog team sometimes went in a whole day. And today, radio
keeps explorers in touch with the rest of the world.

Do you like to read about faraway, hard-to-reach places? You
can because of books about explorers who dared to go to these
places. Now most of the land on the Earth has been explored. But
the bottoms of the oceans haven't—or not very much. And
today's explorers are just beginning to explore space. There will
always be something new to be curious about.

Now you may want to read "Where on Earth?"
under Earth—*also in this book.*

Exploring with Animals

Boats, airplanes, automobiles, and tractors can take explorers *almost* everywhere they want to go.

But in mountains high and rocky, through swamps low and sloppy, across deserts dry and dusty, over snow deep and crusty, explorers need animals to help them explore.

124

If you went exploring, what kind of animal would you choose to carry your food and tools and tent—and to carry you, too?

Would you choose a horse?

Many explorers do go exploring with horses. But some other animals are even better for exploring special places. One of these is the donkey.

Donkeys look much like horses, but they are smaller—except for their ears, which are longer. Donkeys almost never slip or trip, and they can carry heavy loads on narrow, rocky mountain trails.

Another good partner for an explorer is the mule. A mule's mother is a horse. A mule's father is a donkey. And a mule is big and strong like a horse, and patient and surefooted like a donkey. Mules do not become frightened at lightning or thunder. They do not even run away if bullets are banging or if rocks are rolling under their hooves on a mountain trail.

Another surefooted traveler is the llama. Llamas have shaggy coats and can carry loads over high mountains. But when a llama gets tired, it sits down and rests. Don't try to make it get up and go before it is ready. It might spit right in your eye!

What if you came to a *swamp* when you were exploring? A swamp is a sticky, oozy, glubby mud-and-water place that looks and feels like a giant mud pie.

A good animal partner for you in a swamp would be a water buffalo. This big animal looks something like a cow. It can wade through mud to the top of its legs.

An elephant is another animal that can wade with a heavy load on its back through a swamp. An elephant is the biggest land animal in the world. It is so strong that it can butt through the thick trees and vines of a jungle where there is no road at all.

A *desert* is as different from a swamp as anything could be. A swamp has too much water. A desert doesn't have enough. To explore in a dry, sandy desert, you would need an animal partner with feet like soft bouncy cushions. These help it walk across the sand without sinking into it. Your animal partner in a desert should also be one that can travel a long time without drinking any water, because water is hard to find there.

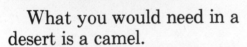

What you would need in a desert is a camel.

Suppose you wanted to go exploring in the far, cold Northland. A reindeer would be a good partner. It can pull a heavy sled over snow and ice.

Eskimo dogs also pull sleds. Some Eskimo dogs look like wolves and are almost as wild as wolves, but they can be harnessed like horses.

127

In the highlands of Asia lives another good traveling companion—the yak. Yaks have long, shaggy, black coats and long curving horns. They look a *little* like buffalo. They can travel comfortably on high, twisting mountain trails, in winds that are as cold and sharp as icicles. If you went exploring in the high, cold mountains, you might want to ride on the back of a yak.

Here are a few rhymes about a traveling yak.
Maybe you would like to make up a rhyme of
your own.

On a twisting trail
With a pack on his back,
A yak set out on a narrow track.
The track was so crooked, alas and alack,
The shaggy yak met himself—coming back.

A yak
With a pack
On his shaggy back
Went for a walk
On the railroad track.
The train came scurrying, *clickety-clack,*
And bumped the yak with a pack on his back.

Traveling a trail
With a pack on his back,
A yak named Jack
Met a yak named Mack.
Said the yak named Jack
To the yak named Mack,
"Get off of this track
Or I'll give you a whack!"
Said the yak named Mack
To the yak named Jack,
"You shaggy old yak,
Go sit on a tack!"

Animals help each other, too.
Read about Animal Partners
under Animals *in Volume 1*

The Lost Necklace

Many years ago a young girl sat as still as she could while a man carved her picture into a large stone in the palace wall.

She was glad that he was almost finished, because it had taken many days, and she wanted to run and play with her brother. Her fingers tugged at the golden hawk that hung on a string of red beads around her neck. She tugged until the necklace broke and the beads scattered on the ground.

130

The carver picked them all up and promised to fix them so they would never break again.

"Oh, I hope you can," the girl said. "They were a birthday present from my father."

After the necklace had been put together again, the man looked for the girl. She was not playing outside the walls with the other children, but her brother was.

"Will you give this necklace to your sister?" the man asked.

The boy took the necklace, but when he saw his sister coming, he hid it behind a small statue. Then he told his sister what he had done.

"Don't tell me where!" she cried. "Let me find it myself."

After that, "finding the necklace" became one of their favorite games.

When the girl grew up, she gave the necklace to her daughter, who in turn gave it to *her* daughter.

Then, one day, there was a terrible war. The people of the city ran away, leaving many things behind. One of the things left was the pretty necklace.

The enemy soldiers knocked
down many of the houses and
some of the city walls. They took
everything of value they could
find. The beautiful necklace lay
unnoticed among some broken
toys.

Slowly, as the years went by,
the drifting sands covered the
city and the walls. Now the
necklace was hidden again.

Each year, the city was buried
deeper and deeper. Camel cara-
vans passed over it, and nobody
even knew there was a city
buried under the desert.

Then, one day, some men came looking for buried cities. A freshwater spring and the way the sand had been heaped by the wind told them something might be buried there. The men didn't know about the city or the pretty necklace, but they started digging.

They dug carefully and slowly. They dug for days and days . . . deeper and deeper . . . wider and wider. Still they found nothing.

But one day . . .

A worker shouted from his digging, "I've found something! A wall!"

Now they dug even more carefully, sometimes gently brushing the soil from the wall with their fingers. When the palace wall was uncovered, they brushed the earth from the young girl's picture. They read her name and wondered who she was.

A few days later, as they dug out one of the royal bedrooms, a tiny red bump appeared in the sand. Carefully, they brushed the earth away until a string of dark-red beads with a tiny golden hawk was uncovered.

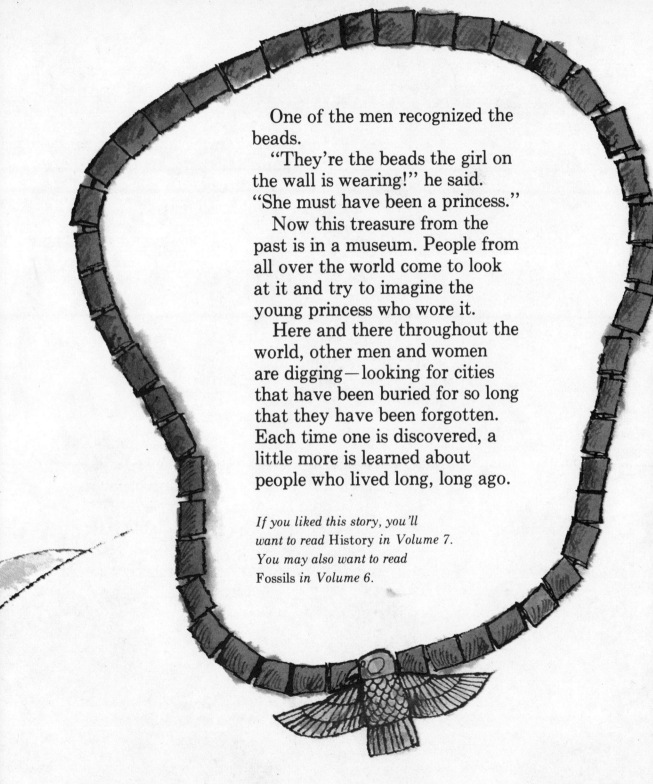

One of the men recognized the beads.

"They're the beads the girl on the wall is wearing!" he said. "She must have been a princess."

Now this treasure from the past is in a museum. People from all over the world come to look at it and try to imagine the young princess who wore it.

Here and there throughout the world, other men and women are digging—looking for cities that have been buried for so long that they have been forgotten. Each time one is discovered, a little more is learned about people who lived long, long ago.

If you liked this story, you'll want to read History *in Volume 7. You may also want to read* Fossils *in Volume 6.*

Lenny, the Spelunker

Lenny's big boots felt very heavy as he crawled along the low, slippery tunnel. He stopped to rest again. The light attached to his shiny hat made jumping shadows on the wet gray walls.

"Now I'm a real cave explorer," he thought to himself, ". . . a *spelunker!*"

Lenny had laughed the first time he heard the word.

"Speee-lunker," he had repeated. "Sounds like a game."

"It's no game," his father had explained. "Exploring caves is fun. But dangerous, too."

Lenny had nodded. "Like mountain climbing, only you climb down instead of up! And it's dark."

Exploring caves was a hobby for Lenny's father. This was the first time he had taken his son on a long cave trip . . . where they'd even spend the night underground.

Lenny shivered a little, even though he wore a heavy jacket and pants. The cave was chilly and damp, and his knees were wet from the oozy mud on the tunnel floor. The cave floor slanted downward, and all at once Lenny started slipping.

He slipped all the way to the wall, and by that time he was buried in mud to the top of his boots.

"Stay where you are," his father called, "until I can throw you a rope." They both laughed as Lenny caught hold of the rope and pulled himself back to the drier rock.

His father made an arrow mark on the cave wall with a thick yellow crayon. He had been making these marks at every turn they took in the twisting underground tunnels. With dark passages leading everywhere, it was easy to get lost.

Still crawling on his hands and knees, Lenny followed his father into a narrow side passage. Lenny had leather patches on his knees and elbows to keep from getting cut or bruised on sharp rocks. The passage got wider and higher, until they could stand up without bumping their heads against the rock ceiling.

As they kept moving, they climbed over wet mounds of smooth rock that looked like giant gobs of melting ice cream.

"Here we are," Lenny's father said suddenly. "This is as far as I came when I was in the cave before." He put his arm out to keep Lenny from walking too far. "Careful!" he warned.

Lenny crept forward and stopped. He shivered again but not from the cold this time. His father was shining his light into a pit that went straight down in the middle of the cave floor.

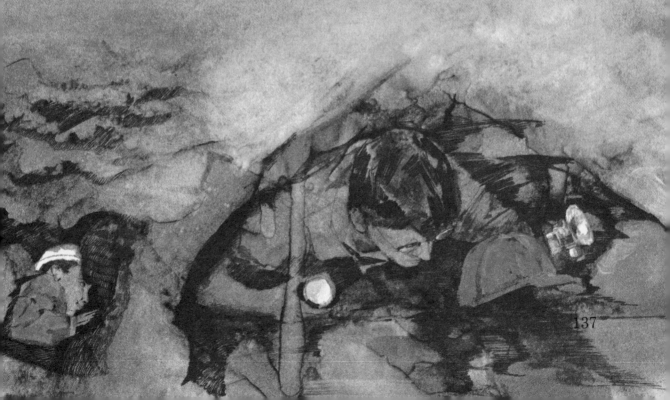

Lenny's father fastened a knotted rope firmly to a ledge of rock at the top of the pit. "Check your boots and pack," he told Lenny.

They carried sleeping bags and food, a flashlight, and, for emergencies, candles and matches. They wore heavy gloves, and their boots had thickish nails—*cleats*—sticking out of the soles to keep them from slipping on smooth wet rock.

"Ready, Lenny?"

"Ready," Lenny whispered.

Slowly and carefully, with the help of the rope, Lenny's father climbed into the pit, while Lenny watched from the top. Then Lenny climbed down, while his father held the rope firmly below. Shadows from the lights in their caps jumped around on the walls of the pit.

"It's kind of spooky down here," Lenny said.

They turned their lights on every part of the deep pit. There didn't seem to be any way out except the way they had come in.

"This must be the end of the cave," Lenny said.

But his father had been noticing a place where it appeared that water at one time had run out of the pit. "Help me pull these loose rocks away," he said.

Lenny pitched in to help. When all the rocks were removed, there was an opening big enough to let them squeeze through.

On the other side of the opening they stopped in wonder.

"It's like we're on the moon or somewhere," Lenny said. "A different planet!"

They stared for a long time at the big underground room they had discovered. It sparkled in their lights like an Aladdin's cave full of diamonds.

"I know there *aren't* diamonds here," Lenny said. "But it looks that way."

What made it look that way were the rock crystals clinging in heavy bunches on the ceiling and walls. Some were no bigger than a baby's finger, and some were as big as an elephant's leg. But they all looked like upside-down icicles.

"We're probably the first people in the world ever to see this place, aren't we, Dad?"

Lenny's father nodded. "That's one of the rewards of being a spelunker—sometimes you get there first. Now we'll eat and sleep, and tomorrow we'll explore some more."

Did you like this story? Read about Caves *in Volume 3.*

A Room Full of Yesterdays

Way up in this house are bits and pieces of a world you've never seen. It's the world of long ago.

This world is in a big room with slanty walls. It's called an *attic*, and it's a place where people store things that they no longer use. Tools, toys, machines, lamps, birdcages, books, pictures, furniture, clothes, dishes, music makers—almost anything you can think of. Things too good to throw away but too old fashioned to use. (It's hard to figure out what to do with things like that except store them.)

These things can show you a lot about what the world was like before you were born. They can show you how people worked and played and traveled.

Let's take a look! There are so many stairs! Attics are always on the top floor of a house.

Here we are! Can you see anything? Attic windows are narrow and dusty dim. Let's wait here by the door until our eyes get used to the twilight kind of light here.

What's that over there on the floor? It's an old-fashioned spyglass, which makes faraway things seem close. Sailors on ships used them to try to find land. Put it to your eye and look through the glass. . . . No, that's the wrong end. Turn it around. Now point it out the window.

And what's that way over in the dim corner? It looks like a monster bird with an ugly green face! But it's only a big wooden cabinet with a dial that glows in the dark—an old-fashioned radio.

Imagine taking a trip with a trunk as big as a closet! People took these trunks on slow-moving trains and boats. When you open the trunk, a smell comes out that *smells* like many years ago. And then . . . you take out a dress that *looks* like many years ago. In attic trunks, there are dress-up clothes for everybody.

If you look around, you may find an old "wooden box" telephone that your grandmother talked into when she was a girl. Instead of dialing a number, she turned a crank. An operator— she was called *central* then—said, "Number, please!"

Do you think that someday your children or grandchildren will be looking at some of your old things? Will they find a newspaper that you thought was so important that you saved it? A newspaper that says—

"FIRST MAN ON PLANET MARS!" Maybe they will wonder what's so special about that.

If you liked this story, you'll like History *in Volume 7.*

How Peter Found the Circus

He could *hear* it, but he couldn't *see* it.

"It *sounds* as if it's coming from that way," Peter said to himself. And he *looked* at the top of the tall brick bank building down the street.

He could still *hear* it, the soft *thump-thump* of a drum.

It was circus day! Peter had saved his money to buy a ticket. But his father couldn't go with him, as he had planned, and Peter wasn't sure how to get to the circus grounds. He *looked* at the warm, bright sun and then turned slowly around, trying to decide which way to go. He *heard* some children squealing with excitement as they skipped down the street where the bank was. So Peter followed them, *listening* for some kind of circus noise.

When he reached the edge of town, where the fields and trees began, he *saw* a tiny flag flapping in the distance.

"That's it!" Peter almost shouted. "That must be the tent."

The drums *sounded* louder now, and he hurried in the direction of the flag. He climbed to the top of a little hill, and then he *saw* the tent. People were crowding toward the entrance. He started to run.

As he got closer, Peter *heard* more noises—a lion's roar and a man's voice calling, "Hurry! hurry! The greatest show on Earth is about to begin."

As he got closer and closer, the noises grew louder and louder. He *heard* grunting elephants and chattering children. The drums *boomed!* He *heard* a flute and trumpets.

"I'm not too late," Peter thought happily.

He bought some peanuts and an ice-cream cone and went inside. He *heard* someone say, "There's a boy trying to eat ice cream and peanuts at the same time."

He *looked* up and *saw* a clown pointing at him.

Peter laughed and found a seat. He kept his eyes opened wide, trying to *see* everything at once. He *listened* to every sound. He didn't want to miss one second of the exciting circus.

Our eyes and ears send messages to our brains and help us make choices about what to do. Without his eyes and ears to help him, Peter would have had a hard time finding his way to the circus.

Our eyes can see things that are very far away—the sun and the stars. And our eyes can see things that are very close—specks of dust.

Almost every animal has some kind of organ for sensing light. Even one of the very smallest animals (it can be seen only under a microscope) has an eyespot that probably senses changes in light. A chameleon has eyes that move separately. One eye can hunt for insects to eat, while the other eye can watch out for enemies.

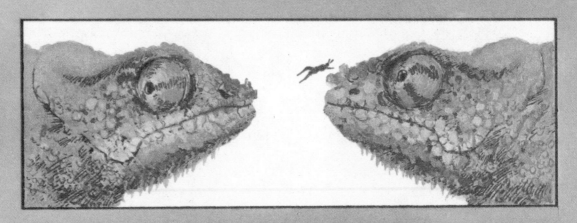

People don't see very well at night. But some animals, such as cats and lizards, have eyes so sensitive to light that they don't need much light for seeing.

A four-eyed fish, called the *anableps,* doesn't really have four eyes. But it lives in shallow water and sees above the water with the upper part of each eye and under the water with the lower part of each eye.

Some animals live where it's dark and have weak, almost useless eyes. The *ears* of these animals are more important than their eyes. Bats send out ticking sounds that bounce off and come back —*echo*—from cave walls or thick dark trees to tell the bats where things are.

A barn owl hears so well—any mouse squeak or faintest rustle— that it can hunt in almost complete darkness. A rabbit is another animal that depends on its ears. A rabbit can't fight very well, but with its long ears it can hear an enemy coming before it gets close.

Some animals can hear sounds that people can't. You can buy a dog whistle that makes a sound that you can't hear at all. But your dog can hear it.

Eyes and ears are two very important learning tools. If you want to feel or taste something, you have to be close enough to touch it. But your eyes and ears let you know about things that are close or far away.

Want to know more?
Read "How We Know the World Around Us"
under You *in Volume 16.*

Eyes That Hear, Speech That's Seen

Mary: "Can you come to the store with me?"
Sara: "I'll ask my mother."

If Mary and Sara were like most of the little girls you know, their conversation would not be especially interesting to anybody except themselves.

But Mary and Sara are very special little girls. They are both *deaf*. They cannot hear. And yet each understands what the other is saying.

How? What would you do if you were deaf and wanted to know what Mary was saying?

First of all you would probably look at the expression on her face. Does she look happy? Angry? Sad? Frightened? Her look might tell you a lot about what she was saying.

But suppose Mary's expression told you nothing. Then what would you do? Would you look at her lips? Would you try to see the words that her lips were shaping?

If you did this, you would be doing what the deaf, like Sara and Mary, do. You would be *lipreading*.

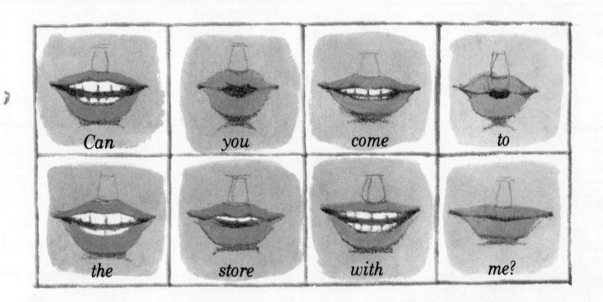

Can you come to

the store with me?

Of course, you cannot lip-read as well as deaf people can. They go to special schools where their eyes are trained to tell them what people are saying.

Children who can hear learn to speak a language by imitating the sounds that their families and friends make. They grow up learning that a certain sound stands for a certain thing.

Mario speaks Italian. Teresa speaks Spanish. Mario and Teresa started learning to speak the language of their countries when they were very young.

But Mary and Sara could not hear the words that were spoken by their families. So how could they learn to speak the words? They learned by going to special schools where trained teachers taught them to speak by *seeing*.

This is how they learned:

The teacher holds up a letter and says the word *letter*. She says the word many times, very slowly and carefully. The children watch her very closely. They study the way her lips move and the way she uses her teeth and tongue.

Now the children try to say the word by moving their lips and tongues and teeth in the same way as their teacher does.

If one of the children does not say the word quite right, the teacher helps by moving the lips of the child.

At one time, deaf people could "speak" only by making movements with their fingers. Since most of their sign language was not understood by people who could hear, the deaf could not talk with them.

There were doctors and scientists who thought that this was unfair to the deaf. They trained teachers and started special schools where deaf children could learn how to speak words and to understand when other people talked.

Many deaf people still use the sign language and "talk" with their fingers. But there are more and more schools for the deaf like the one where Sara and Mary go.

It is not easy to use your eyes in place of your ears. But the deaf children work very hard. When they grow up, they become an important part of the world with everybody else.

Books to Touch and Books That Talk

Almost 150 years ago in France, a 12-year-old blind boy named Louis Braille started thinking about a way to help blind people read and write.

Louis dreamed . . . and worked. He filled hundreds of pages of paper with raised signs that blind people would be able to feel with their fingers. But the signs were hard to make and took too long to figure out.

Finally, an army officer told Louis how French soldiers read messages in the dark of night without using any light at all. The messages were bumplike dots pressed on a sheet of paper. The soldiers felt the dots with their fingers.

Louis was sure that dots were the answer. Dots are small. They are easy to make and can be felt quickly.

When he was only 15 years old, Louis had completed his dot alphabet. Today blind people all over the world learn this alphabet and use it. It is called the Braille alphabet in honor of the boy who had a dream and worked to make it come true.

Look at these dots. They are not big and little splattery dots. They are not here-there-everywhere polka dots. These are very special dots put in special places.

They are all the same size. (The dots in the picture are bigger than the dots used in Braille.) Sometimes just one dot is in a space. Sometimes a group of dots is in a space. Each separate dot or group of dots can be covered by the tip of one of your fingers.

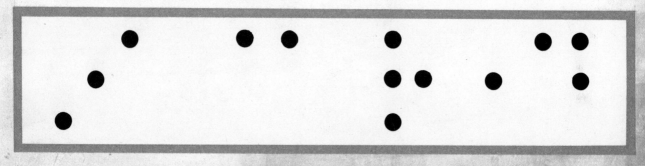

Take a sheet of paper that is just thin enough to let you see the dots on the page through it. Now take a pencil and trace the dots on the page onto the paper. Turn your sheet of paper over and place it on a piece of cardboard. Then, with something sharp, such as the point of your pencil, press down on each dot. Now turn the paper over again.

Close your eyes. You can't see the dots now, but you can feel them under your fingertips. Each dot or group of dots under your fingertips stands for a letter or letters of the alphabet. Can you guess what these dot letters spell?

The dots spell the words *I can read*.

And that's exactly what blind people can do by feeling these dots just the way you felt them. The dot alphabet goes from *a* to *z*. Using this alphabet, blind people can "see" with their fingers!

The books that blind people read have been printed by
machines that make these dots.

The blind can learn to write by themselves by using a special
notched ruler that helps them make just the right dots for each
letter.

Or they can type on a special typewriter that strikes dots
instead of letters.

The blind can even learn to read music by feeling dots. They
can work arithmetic problems, too, with dots.

Another way that blind people can "read" is with their ears.
They can listen to "talking books."

A person sits in a small soundproof room and reads aloud into
a tape-recording machine. When the person has finished reading
the book, the tape of the reader's voice is transferred to a master
phonograph record, from which hundreds of records are made.

These records are shipped to libraries all over the country. Blind people may borrow these talking books at no charge, just as you borrow printed books.

Today—thanks to books to touch and books that talk—blind students can attend regular colleges and keep up with their classes along with the students who can see.

Gail's Best Friend

Gail and her dog, Sam, are waiting for the traffic to clear so that they can cross the street.

Gail is in a hurry, yet she stands patiently, waiting for Sam to decide when they should cross.

Would you let your dog decide when you should cross the street?

You would if you were blind and your dog was a specially trained guide dog.

Most guide dogs for the blind are German shepherds, but just any German shepherd won't do. The people who train guide dogs select only the most alert and intelligent to do this work. And, most important, the dog must be one that does not become easily excited or angered.

When a dog has been selected, the complicated training begins. Dogs that are going to become guide dogs have to go to school. They go to a very special school, where they are trained to do very special work. The dog's trainer holds onto a leather-covered handle attached to the dog's harness. The dog is taught to walk close to the trainer's legs at about the speed that a man usually walks.

The blind person who is going to have the dog attends the school, too. He practices with the dog, and the two begin to be friends. By holding tightly to the handle, a blind person learns to tell from the dog's movements where and when to walk.

It takes a little while before a blind person feels sure that he can trust his guide dog to be his eyes and protect his life. But soon they become close friends.

When Sam comes to a curb, he stops to let Gail step up or down carefully. When there is a hole or an object in the way, Sam leads Gail around it.

At an intersection Sam pays no attention to the traffic light. Not because he's careless but because dogs can't tell one color from another.

Instead of being trained to watch the lights, Sam has been taught to watch the traffic and not to cross the street until it is safe to do so.

This is one of the hardest parts of the guide dog's job. At a busy intersection, things are always happening. Cars come from all directions.

Sam has learned to tell when there is enough time for him and Gail to cross.

158

Sam also knows how tall Gail is. When a branch is low enough to hit her, Sam leads Gail around it—out of danger.

Sam's work as a guide makes him very important to Gail. The dog does her seeing for her. He makes it possible for her to go places and do things without help from other people.

But Sam is more than Gail's guide. He's a friend and a companion. He even picks up things that she has dropped.

159

Credits

PAGES	ART	TEXT
6-7	Keane	Marko
8-9	Suyeoka	Dennis
10-15	Masheris	Dennis
16-19	Thompson	Nims
	Meighan (p. 19 only)	
20-25	Meighan	Dennis
26-31	Murakami	Jordan
32-33	Pulver	Postma
34-39	Fredericks	Nims
40-43	Heslop	Binder
44-49	Kane	Bjorck
50-51	Wills	Dennis
52-55	C. Amundson	Klinger
56-59	Anderson	Klinger
60-63	Joseph	Hildebrand
64-65	Pulver	Riggan
66-67	Taylor	Klinger
68-71	Anderson	Stevenson
72-77	R. Amundson	Dennis
78-79	R. Amundson	Marko
80-81	Fredericks	Saberhagen
82-87	Anderson	Lerner
88-93	Shires	S. Maxwell
94-101	Mitchell	Riggan
102-103	Smith	Buck
104-105	Mitchell	Storey, Zucker
106-111	Joseph	Johnson
112-113	Joseph	Marko
114-117	Kollar	Zucker
118-123	Kane	Johnson
124-129	Anderson	Johnson
130-135	Thollander	Dennis
136-139	Mitchell	Zucker
140-143	Shires	Nims
144-147	Fredericks	Zucker
148-151	Mill	Nims
152-155	Keely	Nims
156-159	Stone	Dennis